THE AUTOBIOGRAPHY

OF

ELIZABETH STORIE.

THE AUTOBIOGRAPHY

OF

ELIZABETH STORIE,

A NATIVE OF GLASGOW,

WHO WAS SUBJECTED TO MUCH INJUSTICE AT THE HANDS
OF SOME MEMBERS OF THE

MEDICAL, LEGAL, & CLERICAL PROFESSIONS.

"Truth stranger than Fiction."

GLASGOW:
RICHARD STOBBS, SOUTH PORTLAND STREET.
1859.

LIFE OF ELIZABETH STORIE.

HAVING a strong impression that injustice is often done to the poor, and more especially to the women of that class, who are more defenceless, both from their sex, and from the greater difficulty which poverty combined with it exposes them to, in obtaining the help of those who are their natural protectors, I have been induced to publish a statement of the wrongs and trials I have been subjected to, in the hope of encouraging those who may be similarly afflicted to put their trust in God, as they too often will find that "vain is the help of man."

The facts which will be brought to light may also serve to warn those in high power of the danger of doing injustice or injury to any, trusting that through the insignificance of their victims the world may never know how much they have made others to suffer.

I shall be well repaid for any little trouble it may cost me to put the story of my life together, if even one sufferer is strengthened by its perusal to bear up more cheerfully under whatever load of woe may have fallen to his or her share. I hope I shall be able to prove to those who may have heard partial statements made in regard to me, and who may have been inclined to judge of me as Eliphaz did of Job in his afflictions, when he says to him, "Remember, I pray thee, who ever perished being innocent?" I hope I shall be able to prove to all such, that, as the "tower of Siloam fell not on those eighteen because they were sinners above all men"—neither have my faults been the sole cause of the evils that have been permitted to fall upon me, and that so heavily.

Of poor parentage, and prevented by early suffering from taking advantage of even an ordinary education, I can offer nothing attractive to the reader of this book except the truthfulness of the statements made therein.

Born in July, 1818, in Centre Street, Tradeston, Glasgow, of poor but respectable parents, I lived with them there for four years in the enjoyment of health and happiness such as I have never known since, but which I have often longed for, and my memory has dwelt upon, as a pleasant retrospect when long months of pain have confined me to a bed, not surrounded by many of this world's comforts. When four years and four months old, I was seized with a complaint common to childhood, called nettle-rush, a complaint which, when properly treated, is seldom known to be protracted over a period of more than a few days, and which is generally completely removed by the use of a little gentle medicine. But, alas for me! under it I fell a victim to the unskilful treatment practised upon me by one whom the Medical Faculty entitled to call himself Surgeon. My father, John Storie, was on intimate terms of friendship with Robert Falconer, weaver, who lived in the same street, and whose son, William, had lately become Surgeon. Dr Falconer, as this son was called, was in the habit of frequently visiting my father's house, and during this early illness of mine, he came in one day while my mother was in the act of giving me sulphur and senna. He asked my mother what was the matter with Elizabeth, (meaning me,) and what it was she was giving to me. She told him what she thought ailed me, and the remedy she was using, but he replied that that was no medicine for nettle-rush, but that he would send up a few powders that would do me good. Accordingly his brother Archibald brought some, two of which were given to me that day. I have a distinct recollection that they tasted like chalk. Many things that happened to me during my early childhood are quite fresh in my memory; for instance, when about three years of age I recollect going with my mother and my eldest sister to see the corpse of Mrs Falconer, the mother of Dr Falconer, who has so much to do with the after part of my history. Mrs Falconer had been an intimate friend of my mother, who was anxious to take a last look at her remains. This visit made a great impression on me. It was the first time I had seen the dead body of a human being. Dr Falconer was in the room. He gave me a sponge biscuit. I saw him lift a plate containing salt, which, according to a superstition common in Scotland, had been laid on the stomach of deceased. The conversation turned on the dissecting-room, and Dr Falconer remarked that he did not care whom he should see there, provided it was not his mother. I am glad to record even one instance of kindly feeling exhibited by the person at whose hands I have since suffered so much, and trust that where a feeling of tenderness and consideration was thus expressed for a mother, the heart may yet become softened to the sufferings of kindred humanity.

But to return to the treatment of my infantile disease. On visiting me the next day, Dr Falconer ordered two more of the powders to be given to me, which was accordingly done. The day following he found me rather feverish, and took a bottle containing calomel out of his pocket, emptied some of it into a spoon, mixed it with water, and kept my hands down till I swallowed it. Like most children, I disliked medicine. The dose he gave to me tasted like the powders, and was of the same greyish white colour. I was ordered a warm bath and cold water to allay my thirst which was great. Dr F. called on the next day, still inquiring if there was any smell, and gave me another powder. On the fifth morning after his first visit he found me very feverish and restless. He gave me another spoonful from the bottle, and again ordered the hot bath. The same evening he called, and I was still more restless and uncomfortable. He did not make any change in his mode of treatment, though the prescriptions he had ordered seemed only to have increased the feverishness and restlessness of my complaint. He ordered two or three of the powders to be given to me daily—the hot baths to be continued—and cold water to drink as before. This treatment was continued for three weeks I think—I continuing in the feverish and restless condition I have described. The smell was by this time very bad, and my head began to swell to a great extent, and saliva to flow in large quantities from my mouth. Dr Falconer ordered me, while in this state, to be taken out of bed and carried round the house in the open air—the snow lying five feet deep on the ground at the time. The salivation continued—my mouth and gums began to mortify, and all my face to become black. My parents began to get seriously alarmed about me—and while they and some of the neighbours were one day standing round my bed and talking of my distressing condition, Dr Falconer came in. After looking at me he ordered me to be lifted out of bed, and asked for a basin. My sister took me on her knee. I did not know what he was going to do, but a sensation of great fear came over me. The conversation about the dissecting-room came all fresh to my memory, and I dreaded something terrible was about to be done to me. While I was sitting on my sister's knee I saw the doctor pour a yellowish liquor from a bottle he had brought with him into a white basin. This was afterwards proved to be aquafortis. He then filled a syringe with this fluid. He asked John Campbell, a person who was in the house at the time, to assist him by holding my hands. He agreed to do so, and while doing this Dr Falconer discharged the contents of the syringe into my mouth. The agony I suffered from this cruel operation was so dreadful that I did not know what I was doing, and I believe I kicked the doctor in the face with such force as to cause him to fall backwards. He, however, in a few minutes afterwards repeated the operation. Part of my tongue fell off, all my teeth and part of my jaw-bone gave way. The pain I suffered was indescribable; but although I was in such agony, the doctor, irritated at some remarks from John Campbell about apparent neglect, went away in a passion and left me without prescribing anything to alleviate the intensity of the pain I was enduring. Some of the neighbours, more humane, ran to the Brewery, Buchan Street, Gorbals, and brought some porter barm which was made into a poultice with carrots and applied to my face. My mouth was soaked with barm sponge all night. I felt considerable relief from these applications. Dr Falconer called as usual next morning, and expressed surprise that I was alive. My father and mother were very anxious to call in another medical man, but Dr Falconer would not hear of it. However they afterwards sent for Dr Smeal, who, as soon as he saw me, told them that I was "*ruined for life by the excessive use of mercury,*" and stated that the medical man who prescribed it must have known the effect of such treatment. My mother told him that I had got a great many powders, but she was not aware they contained mercury, otherwise her child would never have got them. He asked the name of the doctor who was attending me. My mother told him. He said, before going away, "*Your daughter may survive for two or three days, but not longer.*" My parents were deeply grieved to hear this, and anxious to see what further medical advice could do, they called in Dr Litster, who only confirmed Dr Smeal's opinion. Dr Litster called next day and examined the powders, and found that they contained two ordinary doses of mercury in each. He sent for Dr Falconer, and they held a consultation together, the result of which was that Dr Falconer said he would follow the same course of treatment to-morrow. Dr Litster told him he would be doing what he knew to be wrong. They then parted. Dr Falconer called again in the evening. He came up to me and said, "Poor thing, she is far through; however there is a powder I would like to give to her, which is a certain cure;" but neither my father nor mother gave him any answer. The doctor's father came in that evening also, as he had been in the habit of doing during my illness. He mentioned to my father that his son was particularly anxious that I should get the valuable powder he had been speaking about, as it would do Elizabeth so much good. My father did not consent to give it to me, but said he would think of it. Next morning Dr Falconer sent up the powder by his brother, with directions how to give it. The powder was never given to me, though Dr Falconer was under the impression that I had got it. He called in the evening, and observing a jug standing by the fire, he lifted it and asked what it contained. My mother told him it was apple-tea. He said, "Very good, give her as much of it as she likes to drink, but no other medicine. Poor thing, she will not survive long—there will be a change for the worse in the night, however; Dr Crawford and I will call in the morning." Dr Crawford was Dr Falconer's partner. As my end was expected to be so near, many of the neighbours, as well as our own family, sat up with me that night. I grew no worse, though suffering almost unbearable agony. One of the neighbours, Mrs M'Arthur, occupied herself while sitting up in making what was intended to be my shroud. Mrs Angus crimped the border of the cap I was to have been attired in. Both these individuals were alive in 1851, and gave evidence then as to the truth of these statements. Morning came, and I was still in the land of the living, and the place of hope. The powder which was professedly to have done me so much good, having never been given to me, no change for the better or worse was perceptible. The doctor's inadvertent remark, "there will be a change for the worse during the night," seems rather to indicate that evil and not good was the expected result of the valuable powder he had sent to me. There was death in the powder, and he knew it. No wonder, then, at the astonishment of Dr Falconer and his companion in guilt, when they saw that life still animated the body they expected to find rigid in death. No wonder that they exclaimed, "*She is proof of shot*," when the powder they intended for me was afterwards found to contain *as much arsenic as would have killed seven persons!* Even now, when recounting the narrow escape I then made with my life, *and when I remember I was then in the state of spiritual darkness, I feel a shudder come over me.* But God mercifully protected me through that—as he had often done through many other evils that have since assailed me,—and I hope I can now say with truth, that He has done with me "all things wisely and well." Dr Crawford, seeing me still alive on that morning, asked if I had got the powder. Falconer replied, "Yes." Crawford remarked, "She is proof of shot; she will live yet; she has a good eye in her head." This unfeeling speech so irritated my sister that she took the doctors by the shoulders; and when unceremoniously turning them out of the house, Crawford said to Falconer, "If this is the way, render your account—it should be upwards of £20." The remarks and evident astonishment of the doctors that morning confirmed my parents in their suspicions that the powder was intended to have put an end to my existence, and thus to have concealed from the world all trace of the bungling and unskilful treatment of a man who had to earn his livelihood by the practice of medicine. The powder was accordingly sent to the late Dr Lorimer Corbett, Gorbals, who analysed it, and found it to contain as much arsenic as would have killed seven persons. It was then handed to Dr Corkindale, at that time surgeon for the procurator fiscal, who also gave it as his opinion that it contained "*a large quantity of arsenic.*" I began to recover slowly. Dr Corkindale operated upon me, and took away part of the jawbone. The jaw-bones were softened like gristle, and in healing they grew together into a solid mass, so that no support could be taken into the mouth till Dr Corkindale made a small opening which admitted the spout of a tin can, which had been made to feed me through. For some years I was supported by the liquid I sucked through that small aperture.

In the year 1823, the year after Dr Falconer attended me, my father, seeing I was made an object for life through Dr F.'s unskilful treatment of me, raised an action of damages against him before the Court of the Burgh of Barony of Gorbals—Malcolm and Kerr, writers, Glasgow, being agents for my father as my administrator-at-law; Andrew Cross, writer, Glasgow, being agent for defender—Dr Falconer. After several stages of procedure, and proof for the pursuer, the defender was appointed to undergo a judicial examination. He underwent that examination, and in the course of it admitted having administered mercury, as proven, but maintained his treatment to have been skilful and proper under the circumstances.

The pursuer was then allowed further proof, which was led—John Campbell, one of the principal witnesses in this proof, swore to having held my hands while Dr Falconer syringed my mouth with aquafortis. The medical examinators were Drs Corkindale, Balmanno, and Professor Ure. A medical report was also given in by these gentlemen, "finding that Dr Falconer's treatment of Elizabeth Storie was experimental, and that the analysed powder contained a great quantity of arsenic." After this, the case was decided in my favour, and £1000 damages, with expenses, awarded for my support, as it seemed likely I would survive and be an object for life. Those of my readers to whom I am personally known, can attest how the truth of this conjecture has been verified. The defender's agent, Cross, protested against the judgment, under pretence of advocating to the Court of Session. This gave the defender time to get out of the way, and he absconded for some time. About the year 1827, he was found to have gone to Paisley, and commenced practising there, where he still remains. During my life, I have undergone many painful operations, performed by various operators. Drs Corkindale and Balmanno operated upon me several times. As I grew older, my jaws grew together from my inability to separate them, so that the gums always required to be cut away to allow space for food to pass into my mouth. When my second teeth began to grow, I suffered almost unbearable agony, accompanied by the pains of hunger. I often had to leave the house when food was being cooked. It was dreadful to feel the cravings of hunger, and to have food within one's reach, and yet to be unable to open the mouth to take in the smallest bit of solid food. And all this to suffer through the mal-treatment of one who professed to be a physician to those who were sick!

In July, 1829, I was operated upon—the medical men were Drs Corbett, Campbell, and Walker. Some of my teeth were extracted, and part of my gums cut away. Two or three days afterwards I was seized with inflammation in the back of my neck, consequent, they thought, on the operation, and for nine or ten months I was unable to raise my head from the pillow.

The opening made by this operation was about three years in closing, when it became so small that a pin head could scarcely get through it.

In December, 1832, I went into the Glasgow Royal Infirmary, where I was attended by Dr Pagan, who endeavoured to screw open my jaws by instruments made for the purpose.

My father died of typhus fever on 9th February, 1833, and at that time my mother, two brothers, and a sister, were all ill with the same malignant disease. I was the only one in the family free from it.

In 1836 I had to undergo another operation, or die from want, as even gruel, with the grains of the meal in it, could not pass through the space left for my support. Professor Burns, Dr Lawrie, and Dr Allan Burns, were of opinion that nothing would do me any good, except the extraction of all my teeth, sawing a piece off my gums, and removing a part of my jaw, which had fallen under the chin and hardened there, after I was burned with the aquafortis. Professor Burns told me I might survive the operation, but it was more than probable I would not, as I might take fever or inflammation after it was over, and if so, I had no chance of recovery; he gave me a fortnight to think of it, recommending me to commit myself to God, the only sure physician, who alone was able to assist the operator and strengthen me; he also advised me to consult my minister, the Rev. Mr Turner, Gorbals. At this interview, Mr Turner felt it very hard to advise me to submit to so much suffering, with such a faint hope of prolonging my life, more especially as at that time I was quite free from pain; still, he thought I ought to employ the means requisite to preserve life, and if God were graciously pleased to bless them, I might live for many years as a monument of his great power.

Mr Turner frequently renewed his visits during the fortnight allowed me for consideration, as also did many other Christian friends, amongst others Dr Patrick and his father, with the late Mrs Patrick, whose mild, cheerful spirit almost persuaded me to submit to God's will, although I frequently felt driven to rebel.

On the Friday before the April preachings, I intimated to the Drs Burns that I was willing to submit to the operation. It was agreed by them that Allan

Burns should operate, while his father, Dr Lawrie, and Dr Clelland, directed; the time appointed was ten o'clock on Tuesday morning. As Dr Burns' carriage drove up to the door, I cannot describe my feelings, and the struggle I endured; but my readers may have some idea of it. The operation was very painful and tedious, lasting for an hour and twenty minutes. Dr Lawrie's evidence, however, will show their proceedings.

For the benefit of my readers, I may state that I continued for the first four days in a favourable state, neither inflammation nor fever ensuing. Every precaution was used by Dr Allan Burns, and I had the best of nurses in my kind-hearted mother.

On the Sabbath following the operation, the stitches were taken out, this was almost as painful as the operation. For a week after this I was allowed no nourishment, except what was administered by the hands of Dr Allan Burns, through the spout of a small can; he did this for fear of the arteries giving way, which would have proved fatal. I recovered gradually, and in about three months was partly able to resume my former occupation, that of dressmaking and millinery, which I had learned during the intervals of comparative freedom from suffering.

I shall not again harrow the feelings of my readers, by attempting to describe the state of my own feelings, or the pain and torture I have endured under surgical operations, to which for more than twenty times I have had to submit.

After the operation of 1836, finding that my bodily strength would not enable me to earn a sufficient livelihood, I determined to try what could be done to force Dr Falconer, my all but life destroyer, to pay me the £1000 damages he had so long and so unjustly withheld from me. I now employed Mr Niven, writer, Glasgow, to take decree against Dr Falconer. My father had from time to time, since 1823, made application to Malcolm & Kerr, and to Mr Kerr as representative of that firm, to force Falconer to make payment of said £1000 damages and expenses legally due to him as my administrator-at-law, but without any good result. He was constantly put off with promises, and till the day of his death never received anything more satisfactory. I was treated in the same way by him when I applied personally to him after my father's death. I was therefore induced to employ Mr Niven. But Mr Kerr seems to have been strangely won over to the side of my opponent, Dr Falconer, and prevented Mr Niven from taking any steps in the matter, by refusing to give him any information or satisfaction about the previous process, or any clue to it. My own weak state of health and want of means prevented me taking farther steps at that time.

In April, 1838, my sister Jane died. In the following month my mother and I, with the rest of the family, removed to Anderston. I from this time attended the ministry of the Rev. Mr Somerville, in Clyde Street Church, Anderston—the distance from Mr Turner's being too great for me to go there. My eldest sister, previously mentioned, had been married, and died in Liverpool in 1839. On the Sabbath after her death Mr Somerville took his text from Job xxxiii. 24, "Then he is gracious unto him, and saith, Deliver from going down to the pit, I have found a ransom." The word ransom was like an arrow to my soul, I felt the graciousness of God. I felt that he had drawn me many a time back from the pit—but I could not believe that a ransom could have been found for me—me, who now felt myself convicted as a sinner—yea the chief of sinners. Now, how clearly were God's peculiar ways of dealing with sinners proved to me! Here was I left a monument of God's sparing mercy, while many of those, and my dear sister among the number, who had waited at my bedside to see me die, were taken away before me. Why was I left? *This question seemed to haunt me. I felt it could not be for nought.* I went home from church in a state of great uneasiness. I felt there was something wrong. I was a sinner—but where could I find a ransom? I concealed within my own breast the impression made on my mind that day.

B

At Mr Somerville's class, which I had been attending for some time, the subject of the lecture was renewed on the next Tuesday, and on the two following Sabbaths and class nights. On the latter occasion addresses were delivered by the Rev. Mr M'Cheyne of Dundee, and the Rev. Mr Bonar of Kelso. The conviction that I was a sinner, which had begun to be awakened in my soul, was more and more deepened upon me that night. Nothing could comfort me, nor calm my now alarmed conscience. I felt that my soul was dead in trespasses and sins. I felt myself, as it were, hanging over the mouth of a pit—in the jaws of a lion. I longed to be able to say—"I have found a ransom"—but in vain. Such was my condition for months. I tried to find comfort and consolation in the Word of God, but even there, at that time, I could find none. I could not apply to myself any of the comforting passages which it contains. Sometimes a passage would turn up to me full of soothing, but Satan seemed to cast so many tares in among the good seed, that it was speedily choked. I was miserable as before. I could feel at times the graciousness of God in having spared me hitherto; but I could trace his gracious hand no further. With regard to all other surrounding circumstances, I felt as Jacob did, when he exclaimed—"All these things are against me." I made my Bible my constant study. Every spare moment I spent either in reading it, or in meditating on some passage that struck me. The following verses I thought much and frequently upon:—"He came not to call the righteous but sinners to repentance." "While we were yet sinners, in due time Christ died for the ungodly." Sometimes these words brought peace to my soul; but again, I could not believe that Christ could have died for such a sinner as I now felt myself to be. My constant cry and prayer to God was that he would show me all my unworthiness, and also strengthen and enable me to lay hold on Jesus as all my salvation and all my desire. I continued much in this state till the April Sacrament in 1840, at which time I felt a strong desire to join the Church, and enter the service of God as a member of his visible Church. Accordingly, I called on the Rev. Mr Turner, my former faithful pastor, and told him I wished to join the Church under Mr Somerville's ministry. Mr Turner received me most kindly—commended my resolution, and gave me much good advice. One of his admonitions I can never forget. It was, that I ought to persevere, as my soul was awakened to a sense of its danger as a sinner, and it was only by God's Holy Spirit that this was ever effectually done. At my first interview with Mr Somerville, on this occasion, he asked me if I had been led to see myself as a lost and ruined sinner. I could truly answer him this question in the affirmative. But when he asked me if I had received Christ as my Saviour, I could not venture to affirm that I had done this. I wished to be his, and his only; still I could not presume to say that he was all my salvation and all my desire. I felt as if that was too high a position to occupy. Mr Somerville recommended me to wait till the next communion season. I agreed to do so, and continued my attendance at his classes till that time, in order to be better prepared. I read my Bible, prayed, and attended class meetings; but still I could not find the rest I looked for. At times I thought of leaving off this preparation altogether—Satan tempting me by suggesting that if I were elected to salvation, I would be saved without any effort of my own. But then the advice of St Peter, when he calls upon his brethren to give diligence to make their calling and election sure, came to my mind, and I was encouraged to *persevere;* and the knowledge that no one ever perished at mercy's door, led me to wait God's own time for revealing Christ to me as my Saviour. Thanks be to God, I waited not in vain. Previous to the Sacrament, October, 1840, I had another private interview with Mr Somerville, regarding my admission to the Lord's Supper. He asked me if I felt better prepared than on the former occasion. I said I had done all in my power to be so, although I feared my labour had been much in vain; yet, I saw that trusting to God's finished work was the only preparation God would accept of. He asked me if I had yet given my heart to the Lord. I answered no; but trusted that He who created the desire, would also take my heart, and teach me how to walk in his commands. He said I was admitted, and hoped it would be a blessed communion to my soul; and joined with me in prayer to that effect. On the Communion Sabbath, I went forward to the Lord's Table, although much afraid of my own unworthiness, but at last enabled to trust in the spotless Lamb of God.

Till 1843, I remained under Mr Somerville's ministry, attending his classes regularly, which proved great blessings to me, as well as they did to many others. I then joined St Matthew's, under the ministry of the Rev. Mr M'Morland, at the above date, and still continue to attend the same church, St Matthew's, now under the Rev. Archibald Watson, who succeeded him about eleven years since. During all this time, I was frequently attacked by severe illness, caused by my former sufferings, as will be seen by the certificates of Mr M'Morland, Dr Corbett, and others.

COPY OF CERTIFICATE.

MANSE OF INVERKEITHING,
16*th May*, 1849.

I hereby certify that Elizabeth Storie was connected with the congregation of St Matthew's, Glasgow, while I was the minister, and that I had many opportunities of becoming acquainted with her circumstances and character. I consider her a person of much intelligence and piety; and I knew that she was most devoted and industrious in earning her livelihood.

I can speak for what I then knew, and most fully recommend her, and hope that something may be done to assist her, now that her health has failed.

   (Signed) Peter M'Morland, Minister.

I certify that I have known Elizabeth Storie for at least twenty years, but more particularly for the last ten, from the circumstance of her having frequently consulted me professionally, and sewing in many families of my acquaintance. I can with the greatest confidence state that she is a young woman of the best character, and very industrious indeed, as she requires to support herself; and has hitherto, besides, supported her mother, an aged and diseased woman. I know that she has frequently gone out to her work when she required nursing at home. The dreadful state in which she is from all but complete closure of the jaws, there only existing an opening into the mouth which barely admits the barrel of a goose quill, and prevents the taking of any nutriment except in a liquid state, has rendered her now very weak and unfit for work—in fact, unless something be done in the way of operation, the strength will soon become exhausted; and even an operation, I am disposed to think, will do but little if any good, nineteen having already been performed. Under these circumstances, I dare say it is unnecessary for me to say that the young woman is very poor, having nothing to depend on but her own exertions—no relations being able to assist her.

   (Signed) Robert T. Corbett, M.D.

I agree with the character of the Petitioner, as given in the foregoing statement.
   (Signed)
     George Binnie, Measurer, Glasgow.
     Robert Wilson, Manufacturer.
     Jas. Hannan, Merchant.
     Robert Wylie, Manufacturer.
     Patrick Smith, Corn Factor.
     Jno. Paul, Merchant.
     Alex. Anderson, Manufacturer.

I certify to the good character and industrious habits of Elizabeth Storie.

   (Signed) Archd. Watson, Minister.

Elizabeth Storie was connected with my congregation for some years. She left it six years ago. During the time she was a member of it, she maintained an unblemished moral character, and yet does I believe.

     (Signed) Alex. N. Somerville,
           Free Anderston Church.

Glasgow, *June* 5, 1850.

My life has not had much variety in it to induce me to detail its events too minutely. It has, in fact, been a series of painful operations, succeeded by intervals of indifferent health. Never being able to partake of solid food, and unable from the poverty of my circumstances to procure any very nourishing diet—such as soups or wine—I have never been strong. Besides this, I had to work for my daily bread at millinery and dressmaking, and had often to do so when very unfit for it. But God has wonderfully supported me under my many sufferings, and I have hitherto been able to provide myself with the necessaries of life, without the aid of charity.

In 1848, Dr Falconer's sister, Mrs Johnstone, told my mother that he had been left a large sum of money by his late uncle, Bailie Falconer, and that he was going to America as soon as he could obtain the money. I saw that if he was allowed to go out of the country, all chance of recovering the damages would be at an end. I therefore applied to Mr John Kerr, craving him to obtain the original process and detain Falconer in the country; but he shuffled me off as before. I then applied to Mr Patrick Hutcheson, writer, Miller Street, Glasgow, who searched for four days successively in the Burgh Court books for said process, but could neither find it, nor any trace of it in any of the books produced by Mr Simpson, extractor. Mr Simpson charged a fee of one shilling for each book searched, which I had to pay along with Mr Hutcheson's fee. Mr Hutcheson and I went to Mr Kerr, and told that steps must be taken to recover the process or obtain decree against Falconer, and he being agent in the case, was liable and bound to hold Dr Falconer in the country until provision was made for my support. Mr Kerr told Mr Hutcheson not to interfere further in the matter, as he would himself act for the "poor girl," and get Dr Falconer detained in the country—saying at the same time, that "*he should have been hung at the time*, but we did not think she would live to need anything." Mr Kerr then arranged to get a petition lodged before the Sheriff of Renfrew, to detain Falconer, until he could get time to search the Burgh Court books, and recover the process. He accordingly prepared a petition, and sent it to Messrs J. & J. Campbell, writers, Paisley. Mr Campbell presented the petition; but, in whatever bungling a manner it had been drawn up, the Sheriff refused to grant a warrant for the apprehension of Wm. Falconer, but granted a warrant to arrest the legacy in the hands of the executor, which was accordingly done.

A short time after this, Kerr mentioned that he had arranged matters with the Sheriff, who was a tenant of his, and that he would get all put to right. In a few days afterwards, to my astonishment, Dr Falconer lodged defences to a new action, raised by Kerr, *at my instance*, against Falconer. Mr Kerr, in taking this step, either displayed great ignorance of what was the proper legal course to have adopted, while the original process was only *asleep*, or he took advantage of my ignorance, and raised this action, I not being aware of its being raised, or of the effect of such a proceeding.

When I learned the fatal result of this new action, I could not understand Kerr's object in raising it; but from the way in which he has since acted, I have no doubt that Dr Falconer influenced him to try and get the efficacy of the original process done away with. This could not be done more effectually than by raising a new action, as it would virtually make it appear that I gave up all claim to the £1000 awarded to me under that process in 1823. The general reader may not be aware that it is illegal and incompetent to raise a new action, while a previous one is still unimplemented.

The defences lodged by Dr Falconer, with a letter from his former agent, Cross, about the process, are here given.

Falconer, in his defences, says:—1st, He remembers

of being called to attend a young girl of pursuer's name. Her case was treated with proper care and attention. 2d, He admits that medicines for the child were given to her mother, but averred that they were such as the nature of the case demanded. 4th, If they administered the medicine as desired, they only did their duty. 6th, He does not admit, because he does not remember, causing aquafortis to be injected into pursuer's mouth; although it may not be improbable, the application stated was adapted. 14th, The defender remembers of Mr Crawford calling once with him, but does not remember the conversation referred to.

Defender's statement dilatory:—In the year 1823, or following years, an action, setting forth the same grounds, was brought by pursuer, and her father, as her administrator-in-law, before the Magistrates of Glasgow; was proceeded with several stages. Mr Cross, present Sheriff of Dunblane, was the defender's agent in the case; and the letter from him, of the 1st inst., herewith produced, will explain the state of the process.

The following is a copy of Mr Cross's letter to Dr Falconer:—

DEAR SIR,—None of the papers connected with the case are in my possession, it is extremely likely they will be in the hands of Storie's agents. I do not remember whom they were, but the name of the party who has borrowed the process will be found in the note-book, or the receipt books kept for the Burgh Court; whoever gave the last receipt there, is liable. I am sorry to hear that you are troubled again with the *Stories*. If you have preserved my accounts, show them to your present agent, and he will easily understand from them the steps that were taken before; take the same steps over again, and the case will fall to the ground as it did before. I think the action was raised at the instance of John Storie and daughter, who was her administrator-in-law, and as long as it remains as it is, it is incompetent and illegal to raise any new action.

She can take up the Burgh Court process and proceed with it.

You will also plead the plea of *le salo dependance*.

     (Signed)   ANDW. CROSS.

To WM. FALCONER, Surgeon,
 6 Nelson Street, Paisley.

The Sheriff of Renfrew, before whom the new action was raised, granted *Falconer* six weeks to recover the original process, which I, the pursuer, was then to proceed with. The loss of the original process is an all-important point to be noticed here. The proof in it was so strong against Falconer, that it was his interest that it should never again see the light of day; and I have no doubt he paid handsomely to some party to get it taken out of the way. From Cross's letter to Falconer, above given, we find that he had been applied to about it; and he says that Kerr more than likely knew about it. Kerr, though he might know about it, also knew as a lawyer that he was not legally responsible for it, and could therefore, if he were so minded, put it out of the way without any personal risk. After a lapse of three years from the date of the last Interlocutor in a process, it should not remain in the hands of the law-agents, but should pass into the care of the custodier of such documents—the Town-Clerk of the district—whose duty it is to see that such papers are returned and kept in the archives for forty years after date of last Interlocutor. Dr Falconer, as if aware that the process was not in the hands of its proper custodiers, never (as Mr T. Simpson, Extractor of Court, told me,) in any way applied to them for it, or any one for him, though empowered by the Sheriff to do so. Great laxity seems to have been practised in regard to the proper custody of such important documents. There is no evidence that said process was ever returned to the Town-Clerk, after it was borrowed from Mr John Fisher, Extractor of Court, on 22d September, 1823, for which receipt was granted by J. Young for Andrew Cross, Dr Falconer's agent. Should a Town-Clerk be assoilzied from his responsibility for the safe custody of a process, by the negligence with which he discharges the duties of his office?

Mr Cross's letter to Dr Falconer, already referred to, opened my eyes to the nature of the new action, and I therefore declined to lead proof in it, and demanded of Kerr restitution of the original process, in which all was already proven. This was refused. I then applied to Sheriff Alison, who appointed Mr D. Tainsh, poor-agent, to look into my case.

On 19th August, 1849, my kind mother, who had been such an attentive nurse to me during my many and painful illnesses, died. I was nearly overwhelmed by the stroke. A child of misfortune from my earliest years, I felt as if my cup of sorrow was now full. I had been the victim of Dr Falconer's unskilful treatment when a child. I had been overreached by him and his law-agent when the original action was decided in my favour. I was the dupe of my own law-agent, and the sacrifice made at the shrine of the reputation of the man whom I look upon as my all but life-destroyer; and now my only earthly stay is removed—my dear mother dies! I was indeed brought very low by this new affliction.

I had, however, to rouse myself to new exertion. Mr Tainsh wished me to accompany him to Mr Kerr, to arrange about the new action. We had an interview with him, but I again declined to lead proof in it. The expenses attending such proceedings being more than I was able to meet, and besides, I disliked the incompetent action. Mr Kerr, however, over-ruled my objections, by making me believe there was no other course I could pursue till the old process was found, and that, very probably, it would turn up during these proceedings. Vain hope—now, as then—vain. I had therefore to set about finding out those parties who had formerly given evidence on my behalf. This was attended by considerable difficulty from the length of time that had elapsed since the events had occurred which they were to give evidence upon. By dint of great perseverance, I succeeded in finding out several whose evidence I think it best to give verbatim.

PURSUER'S PROOF.

In causa STORIE *v.* FALCONER.

PAISLEY, 4th March, 1850.

In presence of the Depute-Clerk of Court Commissioner.

Compeared JOHN LITSTER, Surgeon in Pollokshaws, who, being solemnly sworn and examined for the pursuer, depones as follows, viz.:—I recollect about twenty-seven years ago, as I think, of a woman calling on me to come and see a child of hers, which was unwell in her house, in Centre Street, Tradeston of Glasgow. I accordingly went to said house, where I saw a child of between one and two years of age, as I think; and the child was suffering under salivation, and running at the mouth. I do not remember the name of the said woman, nor the name of the child; but I found the house which I was directed to call at by the said woman. She mentioned the name of a medical man who was attending the child; but the name of that gentleman I do not at present remember. I do not recollect of the said woman showing me some powders or other medicine which the said medical man was administering to the said child. I do not recollect of sending for the medical man who was attending said child, and having a consultation with him in regard to her case. I remember quite distinctly that the said child was suffering from severe salivation, but how that was caused I cannot at present remember. I cannot swear what was the cause of the said child suffering such severe salivation. My opinion was at the time, and still is, that the salivation was caused by the use of mercury in some shape or other. Had I been professionally attending the child, as is above deponed to, I do not think I would have used mercury to have caused the severe salivation under which the said child suffered; but from unforeseen causes such salivation may have occurred.

Cross-interrogated for the defender—I depone, I think it was in the autumn time of the year that I visited the said child, as aforesaid, and it was in the year 1822, 1823, or 1824. The said child was teething at the time. I recollect visiting said child on two occasions. When a child is teething, it has a peculiar tenderness of its mouth, and when it is teething there is much saliva. I cannot remember the disease under which the said child laboured. The salivation was such that it could not have been produced from natural causes. Mercury is often given to children of the age that said child was. A common dose of mercury would not have produced the salivation under which the said child was suffering. Mercury is a medicine which is uncertain in its operation. Several ordinary doses, at intervals, would produce salivation.

Interrogated.—If two or three medical gentlemen were attending said child without the knowledge of each other, and mercury being a common medicine for children, might salivation not have been produced on the child by small doses of mercury given by them respectively? I depone, If separate surgeons were attending, and each prescribing mercury, there is no question but that such severe salivation may have been produced. There is no doubt that mercury prescribed to cause the effect under which the said child suffered, would have a very detrimental effect on it. I cannot say whether the effects of the overuse of such mercury would be permanent or temporary, and I cannot say that it would be permanent. The said child was a healthy enough child; and was what is professionally called a teething case. The child had no appearance of external scrofula. Mercury is often given to children in teething cases, to abate the fever attending such teething.

Re-interrogated for the pursuer.—I depone, When I

was called to visit said child, I prescribed no medicine for her. I was told that a surgeon was attending said child, but did not understand there was more than one of them, and do not at present recollect his name. An over-salivation of mercury will cause inflammation of the gums, and if produced to a great extent it will cause ulceration; and if an extraordinary quantity of mercury is used, it will cause ulceration of the jaws, and a softening of the bones, and ossification of the jaw-bone.

Re-interrogated for the defender.—I depone, Ulceration of the jaws, softening of the bones, and ossification of the jaw-bone, are produced from cold followed by inflammation, and this is caused by exposure. The said child was not labouring under malignant scarlet fever, neither was the sloughing of the mouth a case of cancrimoris. All which I depone to be the truth, as I shall answer to God.

(Signed)   JOHN LITSTER.
W. S. HOUSTOUN, Commissioner.

Compeared WILLIAM NEWMAN, Surgeon in Stewarton, who, being solemnly sworn and examined for the pursuer, depones as follows, viz.:—I recollect about twenty-seven years ago, and some time prior to May, 1824, being asked by a Mrs Storie to come and visit her daughter, who was residing at that time in a street called Centre Street, as I think, in Glasgow; and I accordingly went to see her, having been previously in attendance on Mrs Storie, the child's mother. The child was complaining. The mother of the child directed my attention to the very sore state of its mouth. I looked into the child's mouth, which seemed previously to have been very sore indeed. It was difficult to say at that precise time what may have been the cause of the mouth being in that state. The impression tried to be made upon me by the mother, was that the child's mouth had been in the state in which it was from the use of medicine, and I could not contradict that impression from the appearances which the mouth had, in as far as such a state may have been produced from mercury. The effects of mercury depends in a great degree on the state of the system or constitution of the patient at the time of its administration, so that a small dose of mercury by an almost equally severe effect in one case, as a much larger quantity in many other cases. An extra use of mercury often causes inflammation and ulceration of the mouth and gums, which is sometimes followed by a sloughing of the parts, and consequent contraction thereof on the healing up of the parts.

Cross-interrogated for the defender.—I depone, The state of the mouth of the pursuer approximates closely to the state of the case of Mrs Storie's daughter. I do not recollect the age of the child at the time of my visit. I only saw the child once. I think she was walking about, but I cannot say positively. I have seen cases of severe sloughing of the throat and adjacent parts from malignant scarlet fever, but never sloughing of the anterior parts of the mouth and tongue. I have seen one or two slight cases of cancrimoris, but have not met with any severe cases. I was not in practice at the time of said visit. I was a student of medicine, and attending medical classes in Glasgow. I was about finishing my medical studies. In certain very peculiar idiosyncrasies of constitution, an ordinary dose of mercury may be followed by very injurious effects upon a child, including inflammation and sloughing of the mouth and adjacent parts, followed by ulceration and contraction of the parts before alluded to; but I have never met with such a case in my own experience. All which I depone to be truth as I shall answer to God.

(Signed)   WM. NEWMAN.
           W. L. HOUSTON, Commissioner.

I do not wonder at these medical gentlemen forgetting, considering the lapse of time since they saw or heard of me, or at their more particularly insisting upon Mr Tainsh finding the original evidence given in 1823 on my behalf, as they could not now state it so distinctly from memory. On Mr Tainsh intimating this to Mr Kerr in my presence, he replied, "I will assure them their original evidence never will be seen." Mr Kerr then requested Mr Tainsh to fix a day to go out again to Doctors Newman and Litster, telling him he would write and prepare the way for him, and that Dr Newman would have a dinner prepared for him, as he (Mr Kerr) belonged to Stewarton, and all his relations were there. Mr Tainsh and I were anxious that Kerr should give him the letter to carry, but Kerr was *too knowing*, and said it would be there before him.

Compeared MARY DUNCAN, residing at Bridgeton of Glasgow, relict of Robert Duncan, Weaver there, who, being solemnly sworn and examined for the pursuer, depones as follows, viz.:—I know the pursuer, and have known her for the last twenty-eight years. I recollect of her being unwell about that time, and the disease under which she laboured was said to be nettle-rush. Previous to that time she was a healthy child. She was attended by a doctor, who was said to be of the name of Falconer, but I never saw him. I resided in the same tenement of houses with Mrs Storie, the pursuer's mother, at that time, and I occasionally saw her. She was, as I think, about four years of age. The pursuer first of all became worse, and her jaws fell. After the jaws fell, her mother got an iron can made with a small stroup on it, whereby she might be fed, as she could not sufficiently open her mouth. I do not recollect that at first the pursuer's head swelled. The pursuer's mother is dead, and she told me that it was owing to Dr Falconer's ill treatment that the pursuer suffered much. The pursuer's jaws are, I believe, still down. All which I depone to be truth as I shall answer to God, and I depone that I cannot write.

W. L., Commissioner.

Compeared AGNES NEILSON, wife of Robert Wright, Weaver in Anderston, Glasgow, who, being solemnly sworn and examined for the pursuer, depones as follows, viz.:—I know the pursuer, and have known her since her birth. I recollect of her being unwell about twenty-seven years ago, and the disease was said by her mother to be nettle-rush. Up to that time she was a very healthy child. She was attended by a Dr Falconer, a medical man. She got worse under the treatment. Her mouth got sore, whereby she was obliged to take her food through a strouped tin-can, which was placed at the side of her mouth where a tooth had fallen or been taken out. She still continues with her jaws fallen, and unable to take any solid food. She is still in a weak state of health, and unable for regular employment.

Cross-interrogated for the defender.—I depone, The pursuer was at that time either five or six years of age, but I am not certain as to this; but my belief is that she was of the age stated or more. I cannot say what was the interval between the taking of the nettle-rush and the pursuer's jaws falling, but it was less than a year. I would not know Doctor Falconer should I see him. All which I depone to be truth as I shall answer to God, and I depone that I cannot write.

  (Signed)   W. L., Commissioner.

Parties' procurators consent that this Diet being adjourned till Monday the 18th current, at 11 o'clock forenoon.

  (Signed)   DAVID CAMPBELL, for Pursuer.
         WM. REID, for Defender.

        PAISLEY, 18th March, 1850.

Diet of proof adjourned of consent till the 9th April next.

PAISLEY, 9th April, 1850.

In presence of the Depute-Clerk of Court Commissioner.

Compeared ROBERT STORIE, Pattern Designer in Glasgow, who, being solemnly sworn and examined for the pursuer, depones as follows, viz.:—I am a brother of the pursuer's. My mother is dead. She died on the 19th August, 1849. She had been complaining about three months previous thereto. I had several conversations with her both before and after she was confined to her death-bed as to the present suit. She told me that when my sister, the pursuer, was about four and a-half years old, she took what is called nettle-rush. The defender was employed to attend her, and did attend her. She complained to me about the mode of treatment adopted by the defender. She further stated that the first occasion on which the defender had called to attend the pursuer, he had asked what medicines the pursuer was taking, and was told by my mother that she was getting salts and senna; on hearing that, the defender said that was not proper medicine for the pursuer to take, but that my mother was to send to his place and he would give her some powders. This was accordingly done, and the powders were given the pursuer. My mother also stated that the defender had prescribed that the pursuer was to take four or five of these powders each day. She added farther, that the pursuer was to receive cold water to drink, and to take warm baths. These medicines and the baths were continued, my mother said, for the space of three or four weeks by the pursuer. My mother also added that she thought the taking of these powders with the cold water drinks, and the application of the warm baths were, in her opinion, injurious to the pursuer; at the end of which period they were stopped. The defender having learned, as my mother farther said, that the powders had been discontinued to be given the pursuer, he, the defender, had called on my father, (who is also now dead,) and had urged on him that the pursuer should continue taking the powders, otherwise, as my mother told me, that the child would be murdered by her not giving them to her. By the defender's influence over my father, the taking of these powders was continued by the pursuer. The defender, on the first or second occasion thereafter, calling at my father's house, my mother said, he had brought with him calomel in a bottle, and had given the pursuer the calomel without weight or measure. The powders also were continued to be taken by the pursuer thereafter, as my mother said, for a week or two, until salivation took place. Thereupon, my mother asked the defender to bring Doctor Corbet with him to visit the pursuer, which the defender refused to do. The defender continued giving the powders to the pursuer. By this time her eyes became blackened, and her head was swollen. After this the defender administered an injection of something like chalk to the pursuer. And after this she had no vacuation, until mortification ensued in her mouth. The defender daily inquired at my mother if she felt any change of smell from the pursuer's body or breath. My mother said the defender used aquafortis through a syringe into the pursuer's mouth, to take away the mortified flesh. The gums gave way, and her teeth fell out of her mouth, and the jaws fell down and united. Before, or about the time the jaws fell, my mother said she called in Dr Smeal, and on seeing the child, and before examining her, he exclaimed, "Good God, the child is destroyed by the force of mercury." My mother said she did not understand how that could be, as no mercury had been given to the pursuer that she was aware of. He repeated that it had been given her. He examined some of the powders in the house that had not been given to the pursuer, and said they contained mercury, and a double portion of it. Mr Smeal is now dead. Dr Litster was then called in; he swore also that mercury had been given to the pursuer, and that she was destroyed for life by it. He called another time, and examined the unadministered powders, and declared them to be mercury, and a double proportion of it that would be given to a grown-up person, far less to a child. He sent for Dr Falconer, as my mother said, and examined the powders in his presence, and asked him how he could administer such powders to a child. He thereupon answered that he would do the same to another child tomorrow. Dr Litster then answered him, and said that if he would do it, he would do that which he knew was wrong. Dr Falconer called after this, and said to my mother that he had a particular powder which he wished should be given to the pursuer, and wanted to know if it would be given, and sent his father to ascertain this at my mother and father. He was told if one was to do so much good after so many had done so much harm, it would be taken. He sent it with instructions that it was to be taken by the pursuer at a certain hour. My mother, having a suspicion about the powder, did not give it to the pursuer; but on the defender calling after the time it was to be given, some person in the house told him she had taken it, and the defender directed my mother not to give her any medicine of any kind, as the pursuer had not many hours to live. He said that he and Dr Crawford would call the following forenoon. My mother told me that they did call accordingly. They walked up to the pursuer's bed-side. Crawford asked Dr Falconer if she had got the powder before referred to, and he said yes; and Crawford replied, with an oath, she had a good eye in her head, and would live yet, that she was proof of shot, in which Dr Falconer, in the same words, concurred. All this I depone to as having been told me by my mother. I am twenty-three years of age. The pursuer is about thirty-one years of age. My mother also informed me that it was in the winter season, and in the month of December the pursuer took ill, and from that time was attended by the defender till about the end of February following. All which I depone to be truth as I shall answer to God. And I depone farther, that the bottle, formerly referred to, was left in the house by the defender, with some of the calomel in it, and it was from this circumstance, my mother said, she came to know it contained mercury. Dr Crawford, before referred to, died a number of years ago; and this is also truth as I shall answer to God.

(Signed)   ROBERT STORIE.
             W. L. HOUSTOUN, Commissioner.

Compeared CATHERINE WYLIE, wife of Robert Macarthur, Weaver in Canal Street, of Paisley, who, being

solemnly sworn and examined, depones as follows, viz.:—
I at one time resided in Wallace Street, Tradeston, Glasgow, this was about twenty-seven years ago. I knew the pursuer from childhood, and I also knew the defender, Dr Falconer. The pursuer's parents resided quite near to me, while I lived in Tradeston of Glasgow; and I remember of the pursuer, when a child, of being unwell. She was then running about in good health, and when I saw her again, her head was very much swollen, and her tongue was also swollen, and sticking out of her mouth in a swollen state. I was told by the pursuer's parents that it was nettle-rush the pursuer had taken. I saw Dr Falconer attending the pursuer during her illness. Upon one occasion I saw him with a pair of crooked scissors cutting away flesh from the sides of the mouth. The defender and the pursuer's father were on intimate terms before this illness. I was told both by the pursuer's father and her mother that in consequence of the treatment of the defender, in ordering the pursuer to get cold water to drink, and to be carried round the neighbourhood in the open air, and this was in the winter season, that mortification ensued. During the time of the pursuer's illness, I saw her frequently, and her parents showed me some powders which they informed me had been prescribed by the defender. That they had been shown to some person who said they contained mercury, and a great deal too much to be given to a person of the pursuer's then age. I remember upon the occasion that I have deponed to, when the defender was using the scissors, of seeing a bottle in the pursuer's father's hands, which I was told contained aquafortis. I was told by the pursuer's mother, that the defender had brought a Dr William Crawford to see the pursuer, one morning or forenoon, when she had not been expected to survive so long, and one of them was reported to have said that she (the pursuer) was "proof of shot," or words to that effect. I have seen the pursuer occasionally since the illness before referred to, and I know that she has suffered very much, and still continues to suffer. And I know of no other cause of her suffering than her said illness or treatment, therefore, as she was previously a very healthy child. I saw the defender fre-

quently in the house of the pursuer's parents, during the pursuer's illness. All which I depone to be truth as I shall answer to God; and I depone I cannot write from recent severe indisposition.

(Signed) W. L. HOUSTOUN, Commissioner.

Compeared ROBERT M‘ARTHUR, Weaver, Canal Street of Paisley, who, being solemnly sworn and examined, depones as follows, viz.:—I know the parties to this action, and I remember of the pursuer being ill when a child, and while her parents were residing in Centre Street, Tradeston, Glasgow. This was in the winter of 1823 and 1824. Dr Falconer attended the pursuer in that illness, and I have seen him and spoken to him in the house of the pursuer's parents. I had frequent conversations with the pursuer's parents during her illness, and ultimately they complained to me of the doctor's treatment to the pursuer; and I was told by her mother there was one powder which the defender had sent, being the last medicine prescribed by the defender: that she was afraid of what the effects of this powder might be, and she did not administer it to the pursuer. During the time the pursuer was attended by the defender, I had frequent opportunities of seeing her. She grew gradually worse. Her head and face swelled very much, her face got distorted, her lips were also very much swelled, as also was her tongue. This I know proceeded from the effects of mercury. I was told by the pursuer's mother, that the defender on one occasion came along with a young doctor of the name of Crawford, I think. And they uttered an exclamation, "Is that girl not dead yet?" or words to that effect. And she told me that this was after the powder had been prescribed, but not administered. All which I depone to be truth as I shall answer to God.

(Signed) ROBERT M‘ARTHUR.
W. L. HOUSTOUN, Commissioner.

Compeared CATHERINE TURNER, wife of Murdoch Morrison, residing in Tradeston, Glasgow, who, being solemnly sworn and examined, depones as follows, viz.: —I had a conversation with the pursuer's mother in my own house, some time before her death, and among the last times she was out of her own house before her last illness; she talked to me about her daughter, the pursuer, and the state of her health—she said that it was caused by the medicines which the doctor had given her. It was Dr Falconer, and that he had given her mercury. The pursuer was then, and still is, in a bad state of health; and it was in her childhood that the said medicines were administered to her. All which I depone to be truth as I shall answer to God; and I declare I cannot write.

(Signed)   W. L. HOUSTOUN, Commissioner.

Parties' procurators consent that this diet be adjourned till the 4th day of June, at eleven o'clock forenoon.
(Signed)   DAVID CAMPBELL, for Pursuer.
WM. REID, for Defender.

PAISLEY, 4th June, 1850.

In presence of the Depute-Clerk of Court Commissioner.

Compeared JOHN M'MICKEN PAGAN, Physician and Surgeon in Glasgow, who, being solemnly sworn and examined for the pursuer, depones as follows, viz.:—I was one of the surgeons in the Royal Infirmary, Glasgow, in the year 1833. I remember the pursuer being a patient there at that time. She was there under treatment in consequence of inability to open her mouth, arising from adhesion between the gums and jaw. This was the most obvious aspect of her distemper, and the next thing was to ascertain whether or not there was mobility of the jaw. Two attempts were made on separate occasions on the pursuer's mouth of operation, but these were quite ineffectual, and did no good. It is quite possible that the extra use of calomel to the pursuer, while quite a girl, might have caused the state in which

I found the pursuer's mouth to be. I formed myself no opinion on the subject, except from what the pursuer told me, as indeed it was impossible for me to do otherwise.

Cross-interrogated for the defender.—I depone, the pursuer at the period above deponed to, was, so far as I now remember, a young girl, but her age I have no remembrance of, although I dare say it will be found in the Infirmary books. The state in which the pursuer's mouth was might arise from excessive inflammation, resulting in the destruction of parts; and there are many other causes for such inflammation besides the using of calomel. All which I depone to be truth as I shall answer to God.

(Signed)   J. M. PAGAN.
W. L. HOUSTOUN, Commissioner.

PAISLEY, 2d July, 1850.

In presence of the Depute-Clerk of Court Commissioner.

Compeared JOHN M'MICKEN PAGAN, Physician and Surgeon in Glasgow, who, being solemnly sworn and examined, depones as follows, viz.:—I now produce one of the journals of the Royal Infirmary, Glasgow, for the year 1833–1834, from which excerpts have been taken at sight of parties' agents, and which is now docqueted and subscribed by me and the Commissioner, as relative hereto. All which I depone to be truth as I shall answer to God.

(Signed)   J. M. PAGAN.
W. L. HOUSTOUN, Commissioner.

PAISLEY, 8th July, 1850.

In presence of the Depute-Clerk of Court Commissioner.

Compeared JAMES ADAIR LAWRIE, Physician and Surgeon in Glasgow, who, being solemnly sworn and examined for the pursuer, depones as follows, viz.:—I have seen the pursuer on several occasions. About thirteen or fourteen years ago, as I think, I saw the pursuer. I was applied to, as I think, by Mr Allan Burns, surgeon in Glasgow, to go along with him to the pursuer's residence, to perform some operation on her mouth; and accordingly I went and saw her along with Mr Burns. On an examination of her mouth, on that occasion, I found that her jaw was stiff, and her mouth could not be opened. We made an operation, by removing part of the lower jaw in front, and thereby enlarging the opening into her mouth. There was auchylosis of the lower jaw, and adhesion of the cheeks to the gums. By auchylosis of the jaw I mean immobility of the joint. The extra use of mercury was very likely to cause the state of the pursuer's mouth, as seen by me on the occasion already deponed to. Exposure to the open air in winter, when there was snow upon the ground, would be prejudicial to the pursuer while under the influence of mercury. The pursuer is unable to masticate solid food, and it must be bruised and reduced into a liquid state before it can be put into her mouth. I think the pursuer might do ordinary sewing work by living on soups, milk, and other liquids, although, as a general rule, the absence of animal food and solids is likely to cause weakness, and injure the general health. I have no reason to doubt the fact, that the state of the pursuer's mouth was the effect of the use of mercury.

Cross-interrogated for the defender.—I depone, Inflammation, followed by ulceration, is the proximate cause of such cases as that of the pursuer. Inflammation may be caused by other means than the use of mercury. The proper and ordinary use of mercury administered to the pursuer, followed by carelessness on the part of her nurse and exposure to cold, would be a sufficient cause to produce the inflammation. My reason for saying I have no doubt that the state of the pursuer's mouth was the effect of the use of mercury, is that the use of mercury being a sufficient cause of inflammation, and she or her friends having stated that it had been so occasioned, I ascribe it to that cause. I have seen cases of inflammation of the mouth followed by partial union of parts, occurring in scarlet fever; but I have not seen in any case of scarlet fever such effects as the state of the pursuer's mouth exhibited, ending in auchylosis. In cases of scarlet fever, the inflammation and sloughing are usually confined to the throat. I have seen cancrimoris or noma in scarlet fever, and in other kinds of fever. And in those cases I have seen a great destruction of the parts, namely, of the lips and cheeks, and bones of the face. The causes of inflammation of the mouth and other parts of the body are very numerous. Mercury is very proper and necessary for children when labouring under certain diseases. It is a very common medicine in diseases of children. It was far oftener used and more freely twenty or twenty-five years ago than it is now. A robust state of health can be maintained by the use of bruised butcher-meat, such as minced collops and bruised vegetables, even supposing the patient is unable to masticate food.

Re-interrogated for the pursuer.—Depones as follows, viz.:—I depone, I do not think the pursuer's disease has been that of cancrimoris. If I had had no conversation with the pursuer or any of her relations, I would have thought the use of mercury a very probable cause of her disease, but any strong mineral acid might have had the same effect if taken into the mouth. All which I depone to be truth as I shall answer to God.

(Signed)   J. A. LAWRIE.
W. L. HOUSTOUN, Commissioner.

The pursuer declares his proof concluded, and signs this minute to that effect.

(Signed)   DAVID CAMPBELL, Procurator
for Pursuer.
DAVID TAINSH.

The Commissioner assigns the sixteenth day of September next for the defender to commence proving.

(Signed)   W. L. HOUSTOUN, Commissioner.

Excerpts from Glasgow Royal Infirmary Journal.

8th December, 1833.

Elizabeth Storie, Aet. 14, Centre Side, 8th December, 1833, ten years ago was afflicted with a skin disease, for which was ordered by the attending practitioner some powders, which she took till her mouth became so much affected as to cause profuse salivation; and at both angles of mouth a spot in cheek about the size of a sixpence became highly inflamed and sloughed, which in granulating became attached to the upper and lower gums, on both sides, which deterred her from using muscles of jaw, which by degrees became so contracted and rigid as to cause complete auchylosis, and now they are observed firmly wedged throughout their whole extent, so much so as to prevent the access of air, except at one small point betwixt two teeth, at right angle of mouth, through which is obliged to suck any aliment she takes; teeth of lower jaw are insinuated behind those of the upper one, and penetrate the gum; lips are much enlarged and unmoveable, causing great deformity; says she can move her tongue and swallows with ease. Masseter and temporal muscles appear to be considerably wasted. No treatment before admission. General health good.

11th January, 1834.

Two separate attempts have been made to open mouth, by introducing an instrument to dilate it, which has been only partially successful. Had a rigor last night for which Dover's powder, the dip bath, and purgative salt, this morning were administered. Complains to-day of headache. Skin hot, but moist. Pulse 130. Bowels have not been relieved. *Injeciatur Enama commune si opus sit*, etc., etc.

13th January.—Feverish symptoms considerably diminished to-day. Headache almost gone. Has perspired freely from the diphontic. Bowels have been relieved. Pulse 104. Skin still hot, but moist.

PAISLEY, 2d July, 1850.—Referred to in my deposition as a Haver of this date, *in causa* Storie *v.* Falconer.

     (Signed) J. M. PAGAN.

(Copy of Letter.)

DAVID TAINSH, Esq.,
 Writer, Glasgow.

The defender obtained a continuation till next Court, and his proof is to be taken on Monday first at two o'clock P.M. The pursuer, Miss Storie, however, is to be out at one o'clock on that day, as Mr Reid wishes his medical witnesses to see her. Yours truly.

   (Signed) DAVID CAMPBELL.

10th Sept., 1850.

Marked.—"Seen by J. Kerr, by morning and by night."

Kerr, having called for Tainsh and found him from home, opened this letter, which was upon the desk, and marked it so. He then sent for me, and said I must go out. I rebelled against this irregular proceeding, of going to the defender's law agent's office for any such purpose.

Dr Falconer having no proof to lead, forced an examination of me, however, by three doctors, viz.:—M'Kinlay, Mackechnie, and Paton of Paisley, who never saw me before, nor knew anything of my former sufferings. This examination was forced in the Sheriff-Clerk's room of Paisley There was no interlocutor granted by the Sheriff or his Substitutes for this act of examination. The following is Dr Paton's evidence:—

18th September, 1850.

In presence of the Depute-Clerk of Court Commissioners.

Compeared JAMES PATON, surgeon in Paisley, who, being solemnly sworn and examined for the defender, depones as follows, viz.:—I have been a medical practitioner in Paisley for upwards of twenty-three years. I have known the defender for twenty-seven years. I have examined the pursuer's mouth while in Court to-day. Would extraordinary doses of mercury, given by the defender, be a likely cause of the pursuer's present condition?—I have not heard of a young person, under six years of age, having been salivated. I do not think a surgeon, in the ordinary courses of his business, would administer calomel to cause such effects as what is in the pursuer's mouth. I can avow for my knowledge of the defender for these last twenty-seven years, that he would not be guilty of giving anything to the pursuer or any other body, to cause such effects as in the pursuer's mouth. I have met the defender both in consultation and in hospital practice, and I consider him well educated and fully qualified as a practitioner, as we are members of a society, and he writes beautiful essays.

Interrogated by the pursuer—I depone I did not see or know anything of his practice while in Glasgow. I do not know anything of the defender's practices in the year 1822, or beginning of 1823. I am in the practice of applying aquafortis to the mouth. Application is made by cotton or caddis dipped in aquafortis, and we tie it to a stick, and rub it against the gums. We are also in the practice of syringing the interior parts of the mouth with aquafortis, through a crystal syringe, that it might not lose its effect, and I myself have done it of late—for the purpose of renewing and invigorating, and restoring the patient to a healthy and vigorous condition of life. I depone I do not know where one of all those patients are to be found, for they are all dead. Over doses of mercury would produce salivation, mortification, and sloughing. A medical dose of mercury would not, nor could not, produce the effects in the pursuer's mouth, unless given in excessive quantities as a poisonous dose. I have never known or heard of such a case as that of the pursuer's.

Interrogated for the defender.—Would aquafortis, applied where there is no disease, produce injurious effects?—Yes; aquafortis would produce injurious effects of itself alone. You will recollect some time ago that there was aquafortis thrown on the cotton-spinners, what effects did it produce on them?—Yes; I depone it produced injurious effects—burning and sloughing.

This is the evidence given by James Paton, surgeon in Paisley.

Additional Precognition of Witnesses for Elizabeth Storie.

Storie *v.* Falconer.

Mrs ANN CLELLAND or ANGUS, widow of Alexander Angus, Blacksmith, Glasgow, residing 27 Main Street, Bridgeton.—Recollects of pursuer when three or four years of age. She took nettle-rush at this time, and Doctor Falconer was sent for. I, being at that time an intimate acquaintance and neighbour of the pursuer's mother, I heard the defender say the powders he gave the pursuer were mercury powders, and I saw him in the house of the pursuer's mother frequently; and I also frequently saw him hand these powders to the pursuer's mother. I know the defender prescribed that the pursuer was to get three or four of these powders per day; and that the pursuer was to receive cold water to drink, and to take warm baths. I know these baths and powders were continued for the space of three or four weeks by the pursuer. I was, and am of opinion, that the taking of these powders with the cold drinks and baths, were injurious to the pursuer. The powders were discontinued, and the defender having heard of this, I understood he called for the pursuer's father, and got him to consent that the pursuer should again commence them. I recollect on the second occasion when the medicine was again repeated, of the defender coming one day to the pursuer's house, when he brought a bottle with calomel, and I saw him give the pursuer out of said bottle of calomel without weight or measure. The powders were also continued for some time thereafter until salivation took place. I think the pursuer's mother asked the defender to bring Dr Corbett, but I cannot recollect rightly whether he refused to do so or not, but he said he would bring no medical man. The defender continued the powders to the pursuer, and her eyes became blackened, and her head was swollen. After this, the defender administered an injection to the pursuer which I thought was mercury, as I tasted it, and I knew it by looking at it; and after that, her whole body swelled, and her tongue hung out of her mouth, and the smell that arose from her body caused me to go home to my bed; and she had no vacuation until mortification ensued in her mouth. The defender used *aquafortis* through a syringe into the pursuer's mouth, I think to take away the mortified flesh. The pursuer's gums gave way, and her teeth fell out of her mouth, and a small piece of her tongue and her jaws fell down and united. There was present on this occasion a man of the name of Campbell, who had said something to Falconer as to the way he was using the pursuer, and the defender threw down the instruments he was using and left the house, leaving one of the pursuer's cheeks cut, and the other half cut, and he never came back till Dr Litster sent for him some days after this. I went for Smeal, who called and saw the child, and he said "Good God, that child is spoiled by the force of mercury." I cannot remember whether Smeal did anything or not. I think Dr Smeal said that no medical man could have prescribed such medicines without knowing the certain result. I cannot be positive whether I was in the house when Dr Litster was sent for. I recollect of Falconer coming one day with a person named Crawford, wishing to give her another powder, and stating that it would do a great deal of good. She said after she had given so many under his advice to her injury, she would give her this one if it would do so much good. And the powder was to be given at a certain time of night to the pursuer. I advised the pursuer's mother not to give it to her child, but to show it to Dr Corbett, and the powder was not given. The defender called at the house after, as he thought the powder was given, and I think he was told it was given, and the defender then told the pursuer's mother not to give her any medicine of any kind, as the pursuer had not many hours to live. The defender and Crawford called next morning to see the child, and walked up to where the pursuer lay, and the defender then said, "Good God, that child is proof of shot. I think she will live yet." "Yes," said Crawford, "I think she will; she has a lively eye in her head," and then they went away.—Dr Smeal, before spoken of, is dead.

JOHN CAMPBELL, Weaver, 8 Bishop Street Anderston.—I recollect of the pursuer, E. Storie, when she resided with her parents in Centre Street, Tradeston. She had nettle-rush when four years of age or so. I knew this from her father; her brother was working with me and I called on a Saturday to pay him his wages; when I was in the house Dr Falconer came in, and he went straight forward to the fire, and ordered the child (the pursuer) to be brought forward to the fire, towards the window, and the bandages she had on her face to be taken off—after this being done he asked me to assist him, which I agreed to do; and he asked for a small vessel and a syringe, which he got, and after looking at the pursuer's mouth he said the right cheek looked "hazardous." I said it did; he then took the syringe and filled it with aquafortis and discharged it in her mouth; after that he took the forceps to lift away the mortified flesh, laid them down again, and filled syringe a second time; after he did so, I said if he had treated that case as he ought to have done, it would not have been so; he then told me to keep the child down, and while he was in the act of discharging the syringe the second time in the mouth; he then went away and left the child as it was, undressed; at this time the pursuer's gums had given way, a part of her tongue and her teeth fell out of her mouth when he was using the *aquafortis*. He went away ill-natured, for my speaking to him as I suppose. When he used the forceps he cut the one cheek more than the other, and he threw down the forceps without finishing the cutting on the right cheek, and went away. I then called in the neighbours to see the state the pursuer was left in. I saw on this occasion mercury powders the pursuer had been getting, and I was shown them on my asking what medicine the defender had been giving her; and her father told me it was these mercury powders the pursuer had been getting all along; and my opinion is, from what I saw of the pursuer, that such was the case; and I am of opinion the pursuer was spoiled by mercury.

Copy of Letter.

Gordon & Meek to Alexander Clelland, Sniggsend, Gloucestershire.

"GLASGOW, 12th September, 1851.

"SIR,—We understand from your sister, Mrs Angus, that you can say something anent the treatment of a child of Mrs Storie's, Centre Street, Tradeston, some twenty-seven years ago, being in 1823, or thereabouts, by a Dr Falconer, who attended and prescribed to her; and in order to ascertain this, we have taken the liberty of writing you, your sister having supplied us with your address; and we will feel obliged by your writing us an answer to this letter, with any information you can give as to the above party. We are, etc.,

"Pro GORDON & MEEK,
(Signed) "WILL. LEITCH."

Copy of Letter received by Gordon & Meek from Alex. Clelland in answer to the above.

"SNIGGSEND, Sept. 21, 1851.

"SIRS,—In answer to your inquiries anent the treatment of Elizabeth Storie, in the spring, it might be, of 1823; she took ill I believe of what is called nettle-rush. I saw Dr Falconer frequently in her father's house, in the capacity of a medical man. She was also taken ill of mortification about the face; she had been some time under the care of Dr Falconer before this last took place; two holes broke out in her face, one on each cheek, several teeth were loosened from her head, while she lost all power of moving her jaws. I do not know that I remember any other particulars. I remain, etc.,

   (Signed)   "ALEX. CLELLAND."

JAMES MILLIGAN, 151 Main Street, Gorbals, Glasgow.—I recollect of the pursuer when she was a child, and she was a stout healthy child, and she was four years of age when I so knew her. I know that the pursuer, when at that age, took some sort of rush in her skin. I know Dr Falconer was called; and I sometimes called in at her father's and saw his child, and this I did frequently. It was the common talk of the neighbourhod that the defender destroyed the child; and I positively believe the defender destroyed the pursuer by his treatment of her. The pursuer is still alive, and is an awful object. There was no other doctor attended the child, and I know this from being her father's shopmate at the time.

JOHN DOUGAN, Surgeon, 7 West Milton Street, Cowcaddens.—I have seen the pursuer, and examined her two or three times, and I am of opinion that her present trouble has been brought about by over-doses of mercury while young in years. She is a complete object on that account, and almost totally unfit to do anything.

JAMES HEADIFIN, residing in 31 Portugal Street, Glasgow.—I lived three years "but and ben" with the pursuer's father, John Storie, in Centre Street, Tradeston; at the end of that period they removed up the street a bit. I had met some of the family who told me little Elizabeth was very poorly. I did not go up that day, but afterwards saw her father and asked me to come up. I saw the pursuer's teeth was out of her mouth, and that that had to be done to let her get some nourishment, and that

Mr Falconer had given her mercury which had caused all this. I knew the pursuer from her birth and always considered her a "healthy, likely child; and I asked her father how he employed such a man? and he said he had been well acquainted with the defender's father, who was an old weaver; and he told me it was mercury he had given the child. I saw the pursuer a short time afterwards, but there was no difference. I asked her father if he had not looked after defender? he said he had gone out of the road. From this distance of time I cannot say whether, from what I saw, the pursuer had lost her teeth from mercury. I have seen the pursuer lately, who is a great object.

JOHN JOHNSTONE, No. 3 Hartfield Street, St Rollox.— I recollect, in 1822, of my parents going to reside in Centre Street, Tradeston of Glasgow, and of their being neighbours to the pursuer's parents. The pursuer I recollect as being a stout, healthy child. I recollect of pursuer being unwell when four years of age, disease I cannot tell. I recollect of a doctor who attended her, but I cannot mention his name, but I think I have such a recollection that I would know the doctor if I saw him again. I had occasion to see the doctor once in Mr Storie's house. I saw the pursuer, and she was a great spectacle and was muffled up, and had holes in her face something like cancer. My mother told me that it was through the surgeon who attended the pursuer that she was so much altered and made such a spectacle, and I heard from common public report that mercury had been the cause of this. The pursuer, who apparently was a favourite with my mother, was frequently spoke about by her, and I have heard my mother say so frequently. She is now dead.

Mrs JANE BARRON or GILLAN, residing at 144 Main Street, Gorbals:—I recollect of the pursuer when she lived with her parents in Centre Street, Tradeston—I was about nine years old at that time. I resided with my parents in the same land; my mother is dead, as also my father. I recollect of the pursuer being bad, and she was a child at the time. I cannot say what the trouble was. I know she was attended by the defender, Dr Falconer, and he was the only doctor that attended her. I have seen him in the house, and oftentimes seen him coming out. The pursuer got a great spectacle while attended by Dr Falconer. My mother, who is now dead, told me it was mercury that Falconer had given her that had made her that, and I heard this also from a great many others; and it was the common talk of the neighbourhood, that Falconer was the occasion of the pursuer being destroyed. I saw the pursuer often in the house when I went with my mother; and I recollect of her cheeks being clean eat away—her teeth was out of her, and she had to be fed with a "sooker," I think, which they put into her mouth.

JANET BALLANTYNE or ALLAN, spouse of Richard Allan, residing at 8 M'Kechnie Street, Calton, Glasgow:—I recollect of the pursuer when she resided with her parents in Centre Street, Tradeston. I recollect of her being badly, and it was allowed to be the nettle-rush that she had. She was then a young child about four years of age or so. I was often in the house when she was ill, from the pursuer's sister, Jane, and I being companions, and from our working together in the same factory. I saw Dr Falconer in the house twice; he attended her during her illness; and I know this from my being told at the time by the pursuer's mother, and afterwards seeing him there myself. The pursuer was reduced to a great spectacle; her mouth and cheeks were all eaten away. I know the pursuer got powders from the defender, and that she was put into warm baths. I saw her when I was up one day just being taken out of a warm bath; and I heard the defender, when I saw him there on one of the two occasions before spoken of, asking her mother about a powder. On the occasion of my so hearing this, Dr Crawford was with him, and they were at the bedside, and I left the house when they were in, and standing thereat. When I so left the house there were other persons there, and the pursuer's sister came out with me. I was very often in the house after that, but the defender was never there; and I heard he had given over calling, after spoiling the pursuer. Jane, the pursuer's sister, is dead, and her father is also dead.

These were precognosced by Mr D. Tainsh. Mr Kerr would not allow into the proof the evidence of more than ten of the witnesses, and thereon closed the record, being afraid, from the precognitions of Mrs Angus and others, that they would demand at his hands the original evidence, as they said it was fresher in their memory then than now. The "additional precognition of witnesses," taken by Messrs Gordon and Meek, parish agents, which I also publish, contains the evidence of those he refused, and contains that of two of the principal witnesses in the first action, viz., John Campbell and Mrs Angus, who held my hands while the aquafortis was being injected into my mouth. Kerr, as I have before hinted, seemed lately more interested in the case for the defender, and by thus weakening the proof, aided in obtaining the decision which the Sheriff pronounced. The case came before him on the 15th October, 1850, when he pronounced an Interlocutor in which he "assoilzied the defender from the conclusions of the libel and decerned," finding the pursuer liable in expenses. As the note to this Interlocutor is rather remarkable, I think it well to publish it in full:— .

"PAISLEY, 15th October, 1850.

"The Sheriff-Substitute having considered the proof adduced, and whole process, assoilzies the defender from the conclusions of the libel, and decerns: Finds the pursuer liable in expenses, of which allows an account to be given in, and remits the same, when lodged, to the auditor to tax and to report."

"NOTE.—Two or three witnesses are brought to prove the mother's statement. They only come in the place of *one* witness—and her statement is incredible—as it is impossible to believe that a person who had had a professional education, and has hitherto borne a good character, should either have used the expressions attributed to him, or been guilty of the attempt more than hinted at, namely, to put an end to the pursuer by poison.

(Signed)   "R. R. GLASGOW."

This decision appears to point to the sort of arrangement made by Kerr with the Sheriff. (See page 25.)

I was greatly downcast at this result, but feeling I had justice on my side, I determined to make another effort to get the law to enforce it. Kerr had led me to believe that after the proof was led the case would be debated, when I could have craved my original process; but instead of this Kerr now appealed to the Court of Session, neglecting the legal form of getting the judgment of the Sheriff Principal. Kerr wished me to go through to Edinburgh and take the responsibility of the case there, but I declined to interfere. So he employed my brother to go as his clerk in this matter, and paid his expenses. He sent the process with him to Mr Stewart, S.S.C., along with the following letter:—

"GLASGOW, 4th December, 1850.

"WM. STEWART, Esq., S.S.C., Edinburgh.

"Storie v. Falconer.

"SIR,—I send you by the pursuer's brother, Robert Storie, a process which recently depended before the Sheriff of Renfrewshire, in order that the sentence pronounced therein by the Sheriff-Substitute may be advocated. Be good enough to acknowledge receipt of the process.

"The pursuer not being in circumstances to pay for litigation, her case was remitted to the agents for the poor of the Paisley Faculty, who, after a very careful examination, reported her entitled to the Poors' Roll, and she was admitted accordingly. In consequence, the case for the pursuer has been all along conducted by Mr Tainsh, one of the agents for the poor in our Faculty, and by Mr David Campbell, writer in Paisley, one of the agents for the poor of the Paisley Faculty; but feeling from the first that the pursuer had a good case, being in fact rendered an object and a spectacle for life by the professional ignorance, if not something worse, of the defender, I have all along taken a deep interest in the case, and in consequence have kept up a continuous communication with Mr Tainsh during its progress. I mention these things to you, to account for the process being transmitted through my hands.

"You will find in the summons a minute detail of the facts of the case, and these facts you will afterwards find wonderfully verified by the proof, when the lapse of time to which the case refers is taken into account. But the Sheriff-Substitute gets rid of the proof at once, by boldly saying that he does not believe the evidence—rather a startling and unusual ground for a judge to assign as the foundation of his judgment—the more especially, when you find that any counter evidence adduced is the result of a brief and unsatisfactory look at the pursuer's person at the moment the evidence was taken. But I need not go into further detail, for you will no doubt examine the pleadings and proof carefully, and Mr Robert Storie is quite capable of giving you any explanation you may require.

"My convictions as to this case are strongly in favour of the pursuer. So strong, that I have no doubt you will at once place her on the Poors' Roll, and ultimately overturn the Sheriff of Paisley's judgment. I am, etc.,

(Signed)   "JOHN KERR."

Mr Stewart writes to Mr Kerr, 10th January, 1851, informing him, that, being no longer agent for the poor, he has handed over the papers, Storie v. Falconer, to Mr J. Macqueen, S.S.C. Messrs Tainsh and Campbell, who conducted the case *at my instance* before the Sheriff of Renfrew, now declined doing anything more in it. They had all along acted according to Kerr's instructions, and, from correspondence of Mr J. Campbell, one may infer that one, if not both of these gentlemen, was remunerated for his trouble by Mr Kerr:—

"17 Gilmour Street,
"Paisley, 15th May, 1849.

"JOHN KERR, Esq., writer, Glasgow.

"Storie v. Falconer.

"DEAR SIR,—This case was on the roll to-day, for parties to meet and adjust. A continuation of consent was granted till next Court.

"They seem to have a claim against you for some neglect in the original case on your part.

"Be pleased to intimate that I will decline further agency, unless say £1 is remitted to me.

"I am, &c.

(Signed) "JOHN CAMPBELL."

"17 Gilmour Street,
"Paisley, 13th June, 1849.

"JOHN KERR, Esq., writer, Glasgow.

"Storie v. Falconer.

"DEAR SIR,—A continuation was granted yesterday to next Court, for defender to lodge a minute, stating whether or not he would abandon the preliminary defence.

"The pursuer was here herself the other day, and on my mentioning that we must have a payment to account, she stated that we were to look to you: that you had promised to pay all expenses, and that you were bound to do so upon some ground or other. We simply stated to her the contents of your letter on this point, and that we would not proceed without a payment to account.

"We are, &c.,

(Signed) "J. & J. CAMPBELL."

"Paisley, 4th Sept., 1849.

"JOHN KERR, Esq., writer, Glasgow.

"Storie v. Falconer.

"DEAR SIR,—The Sheriff to-day, after hearing parties, refused to grant a commission to Glasgow. Proof must therefore be taken here, unless you wish to reclaim against the Sheriff's interlocutor. Should you not do so, be good enough to let me know what early day will suit you or Mr Tainsh to lead proof, in order that I may fix the same with the Commissioner, and give intimation to the opposite agent.

"I am, &c.,
(Signed)   "JOHN CAMPBELL."

After this I applied again to Sheriff Alison, who appointed Mr D. Wilkie to act in my behalf; in consequence of which appointment I received the following letter from Mr Kerr:—

Letter from John Kerr to E. Storie.

"GLASGOW, 11th January, 1851.

"MADAM,—I have just received, per Mr Stewart, the letter of which a copy is annexed. Mr David Wilkie yesterday sent me for inspection, a petition from you to Mr Sheriff Alison, and an appointment of him to act as your agent. I gave him all the information I possessed, and to-day I have sent him a copy of Mr Stewart's letter, with a note from myself, of which I annex a copy, it would only lead to confusion were any other agent interfering. You will therefore understand that, beyond fulfilling my promise to Mr Wilkie, I do not in future interfere in your case.

"Yours truly,
"15 Bothwell Street,   "JOHN KERR."
"One Stair Up."

Mr Wilkie also received a letter from him about the same time:—

Copy of Letter.—Mr Kerr to Mr David Wilkie.

Storie *v.* Falconer.

GLASGOW, 11th January, 1851.

DEAR SIR,—I have just received from Mr Stewart a letter, of which I annex a copy for your information and guidance. I mentioned to your clerk yesterday, and I repeat to you now, that I shall be ready at all times to afford you every information I possess to aid you in your agency for the unfortunate pursuer; and I think I may make a similar promise for Mr Tainsh, who more immediately superintended the proceedings before the Paisley Sheriff.

Yours faithfully,

DAVID WILKIE, Esq.,   JOHN KERR.
Writer, George Square.

It appears to have been Kerr's object to scare off every agent who undertook my case, or at least to keep them so much in his power that his influence guided all the steps they took in it.

About this time my brother wrote to Mr Cross, late agent for Dr Falconer, now Sheriff of Dunblane, making inquiries for me about the original process, Storie v. Falconer. The following is the reply:—

DUNBLANE, 27th January, 1851.

Mr R. STORIE, Anderston.

SIR,—I received your letter of the 11th inst., enclosing copy extract receipt, dated 22d September, 1823. If the process referred to had been with me, it would not have been withheld one moment, and I have put myself and others to a great deal of trouble in order to answer your inquiries.

Your obedient Servant,

ANDREW CROSS.

Mr Cross need not have told my brother that he had put himself and others to trouble, as he had written to Falconer, (see page 27,) that the parties who last borrowed and gave receipt for the process, are liable, and knew that the receipt-book showed him to be the last who legally borrowed the process.

When all hope of recovering my original process through either my own or defender's agents was thus at an end, a counsel in Edinburgh advised me to lodge a summons or petition before the magistrates of Glasgow, craving its recovery at the hands of those they might represent, as responsible to them for it.

In the beginning of 1851, from application made to Sir James Anderson, then Lord Provost, and Mr Reddie, then Town Clerk, an excerpt from the Burgh Court Books (to the effect that a receipt for said process was found given by J. Young for Andrew Cross), was sent to pursuer. The receipt was dated 22d September, 1823. In the same year, 1851, Mr W. Ambrose, Mr George Smith, and Mr M'Donald, all writers, Glasgow, appointed by instructions of Sheriff Bell, applied to the Town Clerks for recovery of said process, but without success. Caption against these parties was also refused. In December, 1852, Mr Quin. Dick, writer, Glasgow, made an equally unsuccessful application to the Town Clerks. He acted by the instructions of Mr Macqueen, S.S.C., Edinburgh, and Mr Charles Scott, advocate there.

Obstacles innumerable were thrown in the way of my obtaining any redress, through implication of the Town Clerks. Kerr threatened to prevent me getting the benefit of the poors' roll, and succeeded, although he had deceived me by pretending it was on the Paisley Poors'-Roll, as in a letter to Mr Stewart, S.S.C., (see page 57,) he professed it to be. He also, in the letter referred to, attempts to apologise for the process coming through his hands, as he was not at the time poors' agent in either Glasgow or Paisley. Mr David Campbell would take nothing further to do with Kerr's incompetent action; and let me see that though Kerr was my own agent, he had been misleading me, and advised me to take steps against him. The Town Clerks said they would accept of no summons. I was driven from one agent to another—from one expedient to another, till I at last resolved to become my own agent. The following certificates will serve to show how very indifferent my health had been, and I was at this time even in a more delicate state. I had been for some months hardly able to work for enough to keep life together; but rather than make my needful condition known, I had struggled on. But sometimes a degree of irritability would seize me, when I considered how all my pain and suffering were traceable to one source—the maltreatment I had received in early life from Dr Falconer. I would then ask myself how it could be that a righteous God permitted me to be so tried and afflicted, while the instrument of all my misery prospered—not only in his profession, but had money from other quarters heaped upon him—heaped upon him as it were to crush his victim more effectually. God's sovereignty was the only explanation to such mysteries.

I was, as in the course of this narrative I have shown, a member of St Matthew's Church, admitted in 1840 by Rev. Mr MacMorland, then minister there, and had been in full communion since that time, attending at the different sacramental occasions, except when the state of my health prevented me. After advertising for said process in the Glasgow newspapers, and making other fruitless attempts to recover the same, I presented a petition on 7th January, 1853, to the Lord Provost and Magistrates, craving them to grant warrant against the Town Clerks of Glasgow for production of original process. Which petition is here published:—

7th January, 1853.

Unto the Honourable the Lord Provost and Magistrates for the Burgh of Glasgow and Barony of Gorbals,
The Petition of Elizabeth Storie, residing at 15 Bothwell Street, Anderston, Glasgow,

Humbly Sheweth,—
That in consequence of the inhuman bodily injuries your Petitioner sustained in the months of December, 1822, and January, 1823, by the wilful and experimental maltreatment, medically and surgically, of William Falconer, surgeon, at that time residing in Glasgow, now residing in Paisley, she and her father, now deceased, instituted an action in the year 1823, before the Courts of the Burgh of Glasgow and Barony of Gorbals, for damages against the said William Falconer, concluding

for £1000; and that your Petitioner and her father, as her administrator-at-law, now deceased, were successful in their suit against the said William Falconer, and decree given for the amount concluded for, with interest and expenses.

That the process in question, which secured your Petitioner said £1000, has been illegally retained, or wilfully destroyed by the Town-Clerks for the Burgh of Glasgow and Barony of Gorbals, or parties for whom they are responsible. She is under the necessity of applying to your Honours for warrant of production for the said process against the said Town-Clerks, as legal custodiers of the same. In the event of the process not being forthcoming, grant warrant for incarceration against the said Town-Clerks, until production is made, or full reparation made of the Petitioner's claims by them. And grant decree for the same, for the reasons and others set forth in the annexed condescendence.

May it therefore please your Honours, on considering this Petition and copy Excerpt from Act Book, kept for the Courts of the Burgh of Glasgow and Barony of Gorbals during the year 1823, certified by the Extractor of Court, T. Simpson, dated Glasgow, 20th January, 1851, and herewith produced, and for the reasons and others shown forth in the annexed condescendence, to grant warrant against the Town-Clerks for the Burgh of Glasgow and Barony of Gorbals, for production of the said process and records kept for the Courts of the Burgh of Glasgow and Barony of Gorbals, with inventory of said process during the years 1823 and 1824, which depended before the said Courts. Appoint a copy of this petition and warrant to follow hereon, to be served upon the said Town-Clerks for production of the process, records, and inventory in question, within forty-eight hours thereafter. In the event of non-production, grant warrant of incarceration against the said Town-Clerks for illegally retaining or wilfully destroying the said process, which, according to law and justice, ought to be in the possession of these said Town-Clerks, Arthur Forbes, Esquire, Angus Turner, Esquire, and William Davie, Esquire, and have deprived your Petitioner of the £1000, interest and expenses, from the year 1824 up to the present date, and until paid; and that till they satisfy and pay to your Petitioner the said sum of £1000 and interest lawful, grant decree against the aforesaid Town-Clerks, they having refused to deliver the process, or give compensation unless compelled. Your Petitioner reserves her claims entire against your Honours as responsible for the Town-Clerks and all concerned.

According to Justice,

ELIZABETH STORIE.

CONDESCENDENCE.

1st, That your Petitioner, along with her father, John Storie, who resided in Centre Street, Tradeston, Glasgow, now deceased, instituted an action before the Burgh Court for the City of Glasgow and Barony of Gorbals, in the year 1823, against William Falconer, surgeon—your Petitioner's all but life-destroyer—who then resided in Centre Street, Tradeston, Glasgow, now residing at 6 Nelson Street, Paisley, for wilful maltreatment, medically and surgically, through mercury and aquafortis, experimented by the said William Falconer on your Petitioner, in December, 1822, and January, 1823, from which she suffers momentously up to the present time, and will until dissolution; concluding for damages to the extent of £1000, interest and expenses; which action was proceeded with at sundry stages, proof led by the pursuer, your Petitioner, and thereafter the defender's judicial examination taken, and finally decree given in her favour, against the said William Falconer, as concluded for.

2nd, That the process in question, which secured your Petitioner the said £1000, interest and expenses, has been illegally retained or wilfully destroyed by the Town-Clerks for the Burgh of Glasgow and Barony of Gorbals, or parties for whom they are responsible, as legal custodiers of the processes belonging to said Courts, and in whose possession it ought to be; and every exertion having been made that energy could do by your Petitioner's friends, herself, and agents, since 1824, at sundry successive applications to the Town-Clerks and Extractor of Court, but were refused its delivery, or anything connected with it, and no clue could thereby be found to the action before referred to, until January, 1851, when the Extractor was finally compelled to search for, and thereupon gave excerpt from Act Book kept for the Courts of the Burgh of Glasgow and Barony of Gorbals during the year 1823, a copy of which is herewith produced, dated 20th January, 1851, and certified by T. Simpson, Extractor of Court.

3d, Although a continual application has been made by your Petitioner, her friends, and agents, to the said Town-Clerks for delivery of the process, since 1851, neither process, record, nor inventory can be extracted from the said Town-Clerks, nor anything from the Extractor of Court, farther than the said extract, a copy of which is produced, which only proves the existence of the case, although the process ought to be forthcoming for forty years after the last Interlocutor given in the case, in terms of the Acts of the Statute on that distinct point, and according to law and justice; and thereby must be illegally retained or wilfully destroyed by the Town-Clerks, as it ought to be in their possession at the lapse of three years from the date of the last Interlocutor given in the case.

4th, If the process is in the hands of any agent after three years has expired from the date of the last Interlocutor given therein, the Town-Clerks are lawfully responsible; but, moreover, after intimation has been given a hundred times and more by your Petitioner, for recovery of this case, and the said Town-Clerks having illegally refused every legal course which your Petitioner was entitled to, she has now no other alternative but to apply to your Honours for the redress as herein craved.

PLEAS IN LAW.

1st, The Petitioner is entitled to warrant against the Town-Clerks of the Courts of the Burgh of Glasgow and Barony of Gorbals for production of the process instituted in 1823, before the Courts of the Burgh of Glasgow and Barony of Gorbals, at her instance and that of her father, as her administrator-at-law, now deceased, against the aforesaid William Falconer, containing the evidence of the wilful, inhuman, experimental maltreatment practised by the said William Falconer on your Petitioner, in December, 1822, and January, 1823; and wherein decree was granted in her favour for £1000, interest and expenses; as the said Town-Clerks are the legal custodiers of the processes belonging to said Courts, and are, or ought to be in possession of the process.

2d, The Town-Clerks are legally bound, after the lapse of three years from the date of the last Interlocutor given in any process, to force return of any such process that may have been borrowed from them, and bound to have them forthcoming at any period when required, within forty years from the last Interlocutor pronounced therein.

3d, The Town-Clerks having illegally retained or wilfully destroyed the process in question, as they have refused inventory and everything connected with it, but the excerpt produced; in the event of its non-production now, the Petitioner is entitled to a warrant of incarceration, until lawful reparation is fully made, being one thousand pounds, with lawful interest from 1824, and grant decree for the same against the said Town-Clerks.

4th, The Petitioner is entitled to production of all records kept for the Courts of the Burgh of Glasgow and Barony of Gorbals for the years 1823 and 1824, that all excerpts relating to the said action may be taken therefrom.

5th, The Petitioner is entitled to the expenses that may be incurred in this action, having been forced to adopt these proceedings for recovery of the action Storie *versus* Falconer, instituted in 1823, in consequence of its illegal retention or wilful destruction by the said Town-Clerks, or parties for whom they are responsible, as any party daring so to do, are liable under a penalty of £10,000.

In Respect Whereof,

ELIZABETH STORIE.

This led to an examination of the Burgh Court Books, where the receipt by J. Young for Andrew

Cross, already mentioned, was found, dated 22d September, 1823.

The process being thus traced to Andrew Cross, application was made to him to return the same; but instead of the process, he sends *copy* of a receipt he pretends to hold for it, signed J. Christie for A. Malcolm. Malcolm was a partner of the original firm Malcolm & Kerr, of which firm Mr John Kerr was now the only representative. It appears rather strange that the Sheriff of Dunblane can now, in 1853, produce copy of receipt he says he holds for said process, when in 1850-51, he writes repeatedly he knows nothing about the process, and even forgets the name of pursuer's agents. In answer to my brother's letter on the subject, he replies, 27th January, 1851—"If the process referred to had been in my possession, it would not have been withheld one moment"—he then speaks of the *"great trouble"* he and others had been put to, to answer inquiries. Strange, that in the course of this *great trouble*, he did not discover the receipt, copy of which he can so readily produce, when called upon, through the authorised examination of the Burgh Court Books. I like to call particular attention to these things; and I cannot help thinking, that if my case had been treated with that legal acumen which is often so searching, I would not now have been making my case known to the public in this way.

The petition I had presented to the Lord Provost and Magistrates was returned to me—that honourable body declining to take any steps in the matter against their Town-Clerks. Having found that the city records for 1823 had gone amissing, as well as the process and inventories of the case, Dr M'Donald, a gentleman who has taken a lively interest in my case, wrote in my behalf to the Lord Provost on several occasions, and through him I learned the result of the petition to the Lord Provost. These are the answers:—

CITY CHAMBERS,
GLASGOW, 12th January, 1853.

Dr WILLIAM M'DONALD,
  Ewing Place, Glasgow.

SIR,—I am desired by the Lord Provost to acknowledge receipt of your letter of yesterday's date, with petition for Elizabeth Storie, and to state that his Lordship intends to bring the matter before the first meeting of the magistrates, which will probably be within a few days hence, and that you will be informed of the result.

I am,
  SIR,
    Your most obedient Servant,
      ARTHUR FORBES,
        Town-Clerk.

CITY CHAMBERS,
GLASGOW, 21st January, 1853.

Dr WM. M'DONALD,
  359 Argyle Street.

SIR,—Your letter to the Lord Provost, and the papers connected with the case of Elizabeth Storie, were submitted to a meeting of the magistrates, held on the afternoon of the 19th inst.; and, as directed by the meeting, I now send enclosed an official extract of their minute, containing the resolution of the magistrates on the subject. At the same time I beg to return the petition, and other papers connected with the case, which you sent to the Lord Provost.

This answer would have been sent yesterday, but from the pressure of other business.

   I am,
    Sir,
     Your most obedient Servant,
      Arthur Forbes.

     City Chambers,
    Glasgow, 25th January, 1853.

Dr Wm. M'Donald,
 359 Argyle Street.

Sir,—I am desired by the Lord Provost to acknowledge receipt of your letter to him of yesterday's date, with the papers on behalf of Elizabeth Storie; and to state that his Lordship having already submitted the matter to a full meeting of the magistrates, and their opinion having been already communicated to you, he has no further answer to give. The papers sent with your letter to the Lord Provost are returned herewith.

   I am,
    Sir,
     Your most obedient Servant,
      Arthur Forbes.

     City Chambers,
    Glasgow, 21st May, 1853.

Miss Elizabeth Storie,
 Anderston.

Madam,—I am desired by Mr Forbes to send you enclosed the petition in your name, which Dr M'Donald transmitted to the Lord Provost, with his letter of 18th April last. The petition is now sent to you in consequence of the request made by you personally two days ago to Mr Forbes.

I am,

MADAM,

Your most obedient Servant,

PETER ALLAN.

I then applied for redress to the Secretary of State for the Home Department, which was remitted, through the medium of the Lord Advocate, to the Procurator-Fiscal of the Burgh Court of Glasgow, that he might inquire into the circumstances and report. His report, made up from conclusions drawn from sources unfavourable to my case, was of little service to me. But still thinking my recourse should be upon the Town-Clerks, I presented another petition to the Lord Provost, through my friend, Dr M'Donald.

On the grounds that the Town-Clerk of Glasgow held a receipt for the process, which depended before the Magistrates of Gorbals, by a party entitled to borrow the process, the Provost and Magistrates declined to interfere. On 8th April, 1853, a caption was applied for against Andrew Cross, Sheriff-Substitute of Dunblane, in terms of the receipt said to be held for process, Storie *v.* Falconer, 1823. Caption illegally refused by Extractor of Court, Mr T. Simpson.

So soon as I received an answer from the Secretary of State (29th April, 1853), and understood that Mr Burnet, Procurator Fiscal, had been appointed by the Lord Advocate to investigate and report—his report was, My case was altogether unfounded; "this!" after the meeting of magistrates, and letters connected therewith—I then intimated and advertised in the *Examiner* newspaper, and put up hand-bills:—

EXTRACT FROM GLASGOW EXAMINER, 21ST MAY, 1853.

Retention of Petition and Process by City Clerks.

"A respectable party states that a petition by Elizabeth Storie to the Magistrates of Glasgow has been delayed, and the Clerks at last consent to give up the petition but not the process. Why?"

Advertisement in Glasgow Examiner, 20th August, 1853.

NOTICE.

Elizabeth Storie hereby respectfully intimates to, and authorises the Lord Provost and Magistrates of Glasgow to immediately cause the Town-Clerks of this city to produce the process at her instance, viz., Storie v. Falconer, concluding for £1000 damages, interest, etc., which depended before the Courts for the Burgh of Glasgow and Barony of Gorbals, which has been, and is, illegally retained by the said Clerks or parties responsible to them; and if by the latter, you are authorised to ordain the city prosecutor and said Town-Clerks to recall the said process into the Court of the Burgh of Glasgow, that she may obtain redress for the cruel injuries which she has sustained.

ELIZABETH STORIE.

15 Bothwell Street, Anderston,
  Glasgow, 15th August, 1853.

Copies of the foregoing Notice, Extract, and Advertisement were duly served upon Lord Provost Stewart.

NOTICE.

AN ALARMING INSTANCE OF THE STATE OF CITY MATTERS.

A Petition was laid before the Magistrates of Glasgow, on 19th January, 1853, at the instance of Elizabeth Storie, residing in Anderston, Glasgow, in which was set forth, that a process at her instance for damages, concluding for £1000, interest, and expenses against William Falconer, formerly Surgeon in Glasgow, now residing in Paisley, for maltreatment, medically and sugically, which depended before the Courts for the Burgh of Glasgow and Barony of Gorbals, was and is illegally retained or wilfully destroyed by the Town-Clerks of Glasgow, or parties for whom they are responsible, and praying that they should be ordained to make the process forthcoming, as well as the records of the city and the inventories of the case: that, in the event of non-production of that process, the Magistrates were bound to grant warrant of incarceration against the said Town-Clerks, or against such parties as they might represent as responsible to them for the process in question, if they held any.

To this the Honourable Body, who are placed to redress the wrongs and injuries sustained by any Citizen, admitted, and still admit, that the process depended before said Courts, but declined to compel delivery of the same in every shape, or give any compensation therefor, or to make example of those who have thus so grossly and illegally violated the law thereon set forth in the Acts of Parliament and justice. Therefore, the wronged and injured now calls in the name of God to her fellow-citizens, countrymen, and the public at large, to aid her to obtain justice for the honour of Scotland's laws; and, by thus furthering the ends of justice, the property of her Majesty's subjects, in her Majesty's Courts, will be made more secure by putting a damper on this art of dodging justice and law.

(Signed)   E. STORIE.

GLASGOW, 359 Argyle Street,
5th April, 1853.

It is consistent with my knowledge and opinion, that Miss Elizabeth Storie's case is one of great hardship, arising, among other causes, from the fact that our Town-Clerks of this city have hitherto delayed, or declined, or rather refused to re-deliver to said Elizabeth Storie her legal process, which is, or should be in their lawful possession, and for the benefit of all concerned for forty years from the date of the action being closed; and, moreover, it is my humble opinion that public opinion, the most powerful engine of the present day, should be made to bear upon the necessity of immediately compelling the Clerks to return the said process to Elizabeth Storie accordingly.

(Signed)   WILLIAM M'DONALD, M.D.

As Mr John Kerr prevented the Barony Parish from taking proceedings against him, as my agent, after their agents took the additional precognitions, the Barony Parish committee found Kerr liable for my support, he having wilfully neglected to recover the process against Falconer, or get the decree put into execution, that Falconer's money, arrested in Port-Glasgow, could have been uplifted for my support. Kerr thereupon defied the committee from interfering in the matter, seeing I had all along supported myself, and never got, nor troubled them for anything; and what they had done and given in this matter, he would pay it all; and that they were to give me ten shillings per month until the case was settled, and he would take good care that would never be. He booked in my presence that he would pay that money, as well as their trouble of paying it to me. And he said it would help to defray any little expense I might be at. Moreover, he offered to guarantee ten pounds to assist me in raising an action against the Town-Clerks and Mr Cross, in the Court of Session; but he must see the draft of the summonses first. I told him I saw his drift, but to keep him out would be as useless as his Paisley action. If I had the means, I would cite all and sundry; but "you, as my agent, are the liable party to me, having bamboozled me so long." Then he said, "You will neither get the ten pounds nor the benefit of the Green Table—try your best." Mr Meek immediately said, "Her charge is against you, and you are decidedly liable."

I was at this time advised by several reverend friends to lay my case before my own Kirk-Session, St Matthew's.

The general reader may not know that the Act of Sederunt affords a parishioner aid in a just cause. The minister and elders of a parish are therein empowered to enforce a case on the Green Table for litigation. The printed schedules annexed, will show the forms necessary:—

FORMULA for the use of Agents and Kirk-Sessions in Framing Certificates of Poverty for Applicants for the Benefit of the Poor's Roll of the Court of Session, under Act of Sederunt, 21st Dec., 1842.

FORM OF CERTIFICATE OF INTIMATION BY AGENT OR MESSENGER.

I [*agent or messenger*] certify that of the date hereof I put into the Post-Office of   between the hours of   and   in the presence of A. B., residing in   and hereto subscribing, a letter or notice addressed to C. D., merchant in   intimating that   is to appear before the minister and elders of the parish of   within the Manse [*or wherever the minister and elders may fix,*] upon   at   o'clock noon, for the purpose of emitting a declaration in terms of the Act of Sederunt, with a view to his [*or her*] admission to the poor's roll to enable him [*or her*] to carry on a law-suit in the Court of Session against the said C. D., [*or*] in which the said C. D. is pursuer. Witness my hand at   this   day of
      Signature of Witness.
                                 Signature of
                              Agent or Messenger.

N.B.—Intimation by letter or notice through the Post-Office must be made to the opposite party *ten free days* before the meeting of Kirk-Session, and a certificate of such intimation returned by the Agent or Messenger in the form above set forth.

FORMULA for the Use of Kirk-Sessions in Framing Certificates of Poverty for Applicants for the Benefit of the Poor's Roll.

We, the undersigned, minister and elders of the parish of   do hereby certify, that on the   day of   in the year   [*giving the dates in words at length*] A. B., [*name and designation*] applying for the benefit of the poor's roll to enable him [or her] to carry on a law-suit about to be brought [or presently depending] before the Court of Session, appeared personally before us, and did in our presence [*if the adverse party or his agent be present, add,* **and in presence of C. D.,** *designing him*] emit the following statement in regard to his [or her] circumstances and situation:—

That he [or she] is   years of age.

That he [or she] is unmarried [or married as the case may be.]

That he [or she] has   number of children under such an age, or in such or such circumstances.

That he [or she] has resided in this parish [*specify the time.*]

That he [or she] is possessed of such and such property [*here specify particularly the applicant's property of every description.*]

That he [or she] is [*state the trade or occupation*] in which his [or her] earnings amount to so much.

That he [or she] has or has not at present any other law-suit depending before this or any other Court, [*or if the applicant has any other law-suit, the case should be particularly mentioned.*]

To be signed by the minister and two elders, adding the words " Minister" and " Elder" after their names respectively.

N.B.—The minister and elders will then add whether the whole, or any, and what part of the foregoing statement is consistent with their own proper knowledge, or with the proper knowledge of any one of them, or whether it is verified by persons known to them, or whether its credit is to depend entirely on the statement of the applicant, and whether he or she is of good character and worthy of credit, or, if the case admit of it, they may add any other *causa scientiæ* that may occur to them.

This information to be signed as above.

The attention of the minister and elders is particularly called to this part of the Certificate.

Although my own Kirk-Session pretended they could not interfere, notwithstanding their Session-Clerk was a respectable lawyer, namely, Mr Adam Paterson, the Barony Kirk-Session granted the remit to the reporters. The reporters refused to admit it on the roll. *Query*, In the event of the reporters refusing such a case, undoubtedly it would be a golden decision to each of the defenders. *Query second*, Has a Parish Kirk-Session even here lost its power? Have they not the power of appealing to the Lord Justice-General, to have the case searched into, and put upon the roll? This is all my own Kirk-Session would have required to do.

The Lord Provost (Stewart) was a deacon in St Matthew's, and a number of the Magistrates were elders or deacons—so we were all members of one body. God's Word commands the strong to help the weak, and so a petition was submitted to the Rev. Mr Watson, soliciting the Kirk-Session of St Matthew's to call a meeting of Session, that an opportunity might be had to take my case into consideration, and assist me by their aid and council. The following letter is Mr Watson's reply:—

Letter to DR M'DONALD.

GLASGOW, April 25th, 1853.

DEAR SIR,—If a simple petition is drawn out for Elizabeth Storie, I have no objections to present it to the Session, but I cannot undertake to read a document which contains so much matter with which the Session cannot interfere.

     Yours very truly,
   (Signed)   ARCHD. WATSON.

Accordingly the subjoined Memorial was submitted by Dr M'Donald to Mr Watson :—

MEMORIAL.

To the Rev. Archibald Watson, and also to the Reverend Kirk Session of St Matthew's, in Glasgow.

May it please your Reverend Sirs,

 I, the undersigned Memorialist, respectfully approach your Reverend Kirk-Session, to entreat your aid, counsel, and assistance with the view of enforcing the honourable Magistrates and Town Council of this City, together with the City Town-Clerks, to deliver to your Memorialist her legal process against Mr William Falconer, Surgeon of Paisley, for the sum of £1000 sterling, incurred for the act of maltreating your Memorialist by said Mr Falconer, who is legally bound to pay said £1000 sterling.

 The honourable Magistrates and Town Council of Glasgow, together with the Town-Clerks, avow, that your Memorialist's process was given to one legally entitled to receive it, and yet the said Magistrates and Town Council, together with the Town-Clerks, decline to grant caption to your Memorialist for said process, in order that she may recover the said £1000 sterling, from Mr Falconer, in terms of the said process, now retained as explained by your Memorialist.

 I therefore humbly pray your Reverend Court to aid your Memorialist to compel delivery of the process, or to recover the £1000 sterling concluded for in said process.

 And your Memorialist shall ever pray.

          ELIZABETH STORIE.

15 Bothwell Street, Glasgow,
 May, 1853.

See the Confession of Faith, Larger Catechism, page 314, Question 141, and Answer, with Scripture proofs thereon.

See the Confession of Faith, Shorter Catechism, page 426, Question 74, and Answer, with Scripture proofs thereon.

See the Confession of Faith, the form of Church Government, page 573, Article First.

The following is his answer:—

GLASGOW, June 20, 1853.

MY DEAR SIR,—It is found that the Kirk-Session can do nothing in the case of Elizabeth Storie. I am sorry for the distressed condition of her body. I think it would be well if she could receive permanent and sufficient relief from the funds of the Barony parish.

I am,
Very truly yours,
ARCHIBALD WATSON.

Mr Watson did not formally lay the petition before his Kirk Session, as he promised to do, so I wrote to him reminding him of his promise, and stating that Mr Wylie and Mr Carr, who were present at the meeting referred to, had neither seen nor heard of such a matter; and had he brought it forward, something would have been done, as they said they all knew me; to which letter the following is Mr Watson's reply:—

Copy Letter.

DR M'DONALD.

GLASGOW, June 26th, 1853.

MY DEAR SIR,—In consequence of a letter, signed by Elizabeth Storie, which I received yesterday, it may be

F

right to explain to you about the petition. I told you I would bring it before the Session, and at the last meeting I intended to read it. In the course of the evening, however, I found to my regret that I had forgotten it; but I communicated the substance of it to the members present, and afterwards to some who were absent, and the result is as I stated in my former note. If it would be more satisfactory to have a formal deliverance, that may be had at next meeting. Perhaps I ought, in courtesy to yourself, as a gentleman who has taken a deep interest in Miss Storie's case, to have explained the violation of *the letter* of my word to you, and if so, I am sure you will accept of my apology. At the same time you will believe me when I say that the spirit of that promise was kept.

I am,

My dear Sir,

Very faithfully yours,

ARCHIBALD WATSON.

The many annoyances that had lately come so rapidly one after the other upon me, threw me into a very weak state of health. I was confined almost entirely to bed for some months; this weakness was attended with severe palpitation of the heart. I sometimes fell into a kind of dumb stupor, and was consequently unable to work. I felt the loss of not being able to go to church, but the doctors prohibited me from going there while I was in that weak state; however I sometimes ventured out of a Sabbath when I felt a little stronger. But one Sabbath that I had gone to St Matthew's, in the month of July, 1853, I took ill and was brought home by two of the doorkeepers. The first thing that I remember, on returning to consciousness, was seeing Dr Joshua Paterson, and then hearing him say to some of the neighbours who had gathered round me: "Poor thing, her struggles will soon be over." I, however, rallied again. Mr Allen, the missionary, had preached that day for Mr Watson. He called the next evening to inquire for me, and regretted he had not known before that there was such a delicate person in the congregation, as he would have been to see me before. He told me Mr Watson was from home, but that he expected him next day and would tell him about me, and he would likely come and see me on Wednesday. I was indeed much in need of a friend. I had been seized on that Sabbath with inflammation in the side, and my condition was truly very miserable. I looked forward with pleasure to the day when I might have a visit of consolation from my pastor; but instead of coming, he sent Mr Allen on the following Monday to say that he had no right to visit me, and that it was ill-done of me to expect a visit from him, as he did not know me as a member of his church. Unable to work, neither food nor fire, nor money to procure them either, was in my power. I cannot find words at present to express my anguish of soul and body when this hard-hearted message was delivered to me. For the first and only time in my life, I sinfully wished I had got the powder containing the arsenic Falconer intended for me. Mr Allen being recently appointed missionary to St Matthew's, I thought there might be some mistake, so I gave him the certificate I had got from Mr M'Morland, before inserted, and the following :—

GLASGOW, 29th January, 1851.

I certify that Elizabeth Storie has been a member of St Matthew's Church for some years. She has, during all that time, been in very poor health. She supported herself by dressmaking, and was very industrious; and, I believe, always well-behaved.

JAS. HANNAN, Elder.

I concur in the above certificate.
ADAM PATERSON, Elder.
ARCH. WATSON, Minister, St Matthew's.

This seemed to satisfy him that there was a mistake somewhere, adding, "No one durst take your name off the roll." But in the month of October of that year, I found to my great astonishment that there had been no mistake on Mr Allen's part, but that Mr Watson, for some unaccountable reason, had removed my name from the communion roll—for on applying in the usual form for a token at that communion season —Mr Collie, the officiating elder for the district in which I sat, refused to give me one, telling me I would require to apply to Mr Watson, and that I would find him in the session-house. I accordingly went there and found him; Mr Carr and Mr Balderston were also present. I stated to Mr Watson that I had been refused a token, and had been sent to him. The reason of the refusal I did not know. He then said, "You cannot get a token, as you do not belong to this congregation, and have no claim here; besides, you are not in a proper state of mind to receive a token, and will not get one here." I therefore requested him to fix a meeting of Session, that I might have an opportunity of hearing any charge he might have against me, as I thought I was able as I was willing to satisfy them. Mr Watson replied he had not time to call a meeting of Session, nor could he be troubled with me. I then reminded him of his sacred office, and told him I thought he was bound to call a meeting of Session that I might be charged and heard—or to give me a token or written charge—I would accept of one or other. He then desired me to take a seat till he would fix a meeting of Session. By this time there were six elders present. Mr Watson turned to Mr Paterson, Session-Clerk, and to my astonishment, I heard Mr Watson say to him—"Would you go forward and refuse her a token?" Mr Paterson replied that he *would not*, and left the session-house. Mr Watson then asked Mr Balderston, who had been looking on all the while, if he would refuse me one. He said, "I will not; she has craved a meeting of Session; if you have any charge against her, fix the meeting, and I will interfere there." Mr Watson said he had no charge against me, and therefore could fix no meeting. He then asked Mr Hannan to give me a refusal, but he merely shook his head. Dr Moses Buchanan was coming in, when Mr Watson asked him to go forward and speak to me, and he would see that I was in a state of perfect insanity. The doctor said, "Oh yes, I'll just do that." All I could get uttered to my God in secret was—"Lord protect me from the fowler's snare, and from the hands of mine enemies." By this time the doctor was standing beside me; but God had heard and answered the prayer of the needy, and the doctor had no word to speak. He looked earnestly at me, but could say nothing. He left me, and going to Mr Watson, who was outside of the door, said, in a loud voice, "I will do nothing of the kind." Mr Hannan then called me aside into the church, and told me I could get no token there as I did not belong to that church. I asked him to what church I belonged, as I would go there on his recommendation. He did not know, he said; that was for me to find out. I again asked a token, a written charge, or the promised meeting of Session, that I might be heard in my own defence, as a member of the Church of Scotland was entitled to be. He replied that I could get none of my requests—they knew better. But if I wished to join that church, I must come as a young communicant. I followed him into the session-house. Mr M'Morland, who had preached that afternoon, was there now. I repeated my former request. Mr Hannan said—"Go away with you; you will get neither a token, charge, nor hearing; go away now; I say you'll get nothing here." I then handed him my Bible, and requested him to find to me, if he could, the passage in it where Jesus said to his disciples—"Go away; you can get nothing from me." I then turned, and referring to Mr M'Morland said—"What a change since he left!" Mr Hannan attempted to push me out of the door; but Dr Buchanan interfered and prevented that act from being committed. Mr Hannan had been exalted at that time to the office of Dean of Guild, and may be excused for having forgotten for a moment that he did not reign supreme everywhere. That evening I wrote to the Rev. Mr Watson, craving an appointment of the promised meeting of Session, a written charge, or a token, and an answer was waited for. He sent his servant to say "there was no answer to the note." I then called on Dr Moses Buchanan to know the reason I was thus informally dealt with. He stated that he was an honest man, and told the truth; the impression tried to be made upon him was that I was in a state of perfect insanity—but this he neither could nor would state—and repeated the assertion that he was an honest man, and told the truth. At next communion season I again applied for a token with the same result. My applications to both minister and elders were alike unheeded; from motives best known to themselves, they were treated with silent contempt. Being thus deprived of church privileges, and at a time when the law had almost left me without hope of redress from its Courts, I felt indeed very depressed. I was certainly not in a very comfortable state in my outward circumstances, and needed all the more the soothing consolations which are often found in attendance on the ordinances of religion, and which they are suited to afford. The three learned professions are now marshalled against me; law and medicine had had their time, and now the church follows in their train. By my very birth —the daughter of a tradesman—a barrier seems to have been placed between me and my formidable opponents. Shall I then go down to the grave a victim to the three learned professions? It is one's duty to submit without a murmur to heavy grievances, when these come directly from the hand of God; but in my case, where man seems to have lorded it over a poor afflicted creature, with none to help her, I think, when God gives the energy of mind to combat with the foe, it is equally one's duty to use their energies in the assertion of what is just and right. Moses asserted the rights of the Israelites when oppressed by Pharoah. Job contended with his friends for the right; and Samson died in the service of his oppressed countrymen. I may be told that my position is different. I am contending solely for my own ends; but no—for if the Church is made to feel that its weak members are liable to be oppressed by the strong, she may be stirred up to greater vigilance to watch over their interests; and I am confident that good will accrue to *many* from the publication of the treatment I received from the Kirk-Session of St Matthew's and the Presbytery of Glasgow.

Impelled by such motives, I saw it my duty to present a petition, February, 1854, to the Kirk Session of St Matthew's, praying for an explanation of their treatment, and craving extracts of charge, evidence, and sentence of excommunication to be furnished to me—petitioner.

The petition was not taken up by the reverend body, till 4th April, 1854. In March, when the petition should have been taken up, I went to the session-house accompanied by a friend. Our appearance was intimated to the Session, but we were not admitted, as Mr M'Kinlay, one of its members, told us that no petition had been lodged there—the petition had been entrusted to Mr Paterson, Session Clerk, who was not present at this time. On 4th April we went again to the session-house. My petition had been presented, but we were told the Session could not entertain it. Mr Watson, in an unbecoming tone of voice, demanded of me to speak and tell what I wanted. I was at this time very weak, and unable to speak in consequence of another piece of my jaw-bone having given way and lodged in my throat, a few days previously. (This had happened while I was in the country; and as soon as my struggling agony was observed by the members of the family I was staying with, the gardener was despatched for the nearest medical aid. As the doctor arrived, I swallowed the piece of bone, which gave me indescribable relief, but left me at the time in a very precarious condition, and very unable for the exertion of speaking.) As well as I could, therefore, I pleaded my weakness and inability to speak, and craved to be heard through my friend; but Mr Watson requested me to be seated for a little, and said, "Perhaps you will be able to speak in a few minutes." After a short time he asked me if I felt better, and was able to speak. I replied, "No; but if they would read my petition it would explain all." Mr Watson said there was no petition on the table. I happened to have a copy of it with me, so I placed it on the table, and it was then read by Mr White, who acted as Clerk.

No one in the Session took any share in the matter except Mr Watson, who thus became both my accuser and judge. Mr Watson suggested that if I asked communion, then, in proper form, they would receive me as a young communicant; but being already a member of the church, I decidedly refused to deny my first covenant vow with my Saviour. I took instruments, protested, and appealed to the Presbytery. But before lodging my complaint with that reverend body, I called, by Rev. Dr Muir's advice, on Mr Watson, and beseeched him, as a faithful shepherd of God's flock, to point out to me, if he detected in me any error of doctrine, or any piece of conduct unbecoming a follower of Christ, that I might give satisfaction to the church, as I was willing to submit to church discipline, if such was the case. I told him I thought him responsible, if he detected a fault in me, and punished me for it, by withholding from me church privileges, without telling me what that fault was. He told me he did not think I had been so well informed on such matters, otherwise the former proceedings would not have taken place. I replied that that was no excuse: he was under a solemn vow to be a teacher to the unlearned, and it was well for him that his treatment had not been practised upon one less experienced. It might have driven some to a perfect hatred of religion, but for me it was only driving me closer to my Saviour. Many a rough and thorny path leads the sinner home to God.

Mr Watson said I at present held no place in the church, but he was quite satisfied, and had no objection now to receive me as a young communicant. This I again positively objected to.

There was nothing else for me to do, but to lodge a petition with the Presbytery at their meeting in August, 1854. My petition was read at their meeting then, but the consideration of it was postponed till 6th September. The following is a copy of that petition:—

>Unto the Reverend the Presbytery of Glasgow,
>
>The Petition and Appeal of Elizabeth Storie, residing in No. 15 Bothwell Street, Glasgow,

Humbly Sheweth,—

That your Petitioner was admitted a visible member of St Matthew's Church Congregation, at the dispensing of the Sacramental Ordinance of the Lord's Supper in the Autumn of 1842, and she continued a communicating member of that congregation until October, 1853, when upon applying on the Fast Day, in the usual way, for a token to admit to the Lord's Table on the following Sabbath, 23d October last, to participate in the privilege of Communion as formerly, she was refused in an unfeeling and unchristianlike manner, both by the Rev. Mr Watson, the minister of St Matthew's Church, and by Mr James Hannan, an officiating elder thereof.

That the conduct of these parties towards her, and the refusal of the token applied for, was unaccompanied by any charge against the petitioner's moral character, or any explanation whatever; and although she requested, by letters addressed to the Rev. Mr Watson and others, to state the cause of their conduct and of her excommunication from church privileges, her application has been treated with silent contempt, or for other motives best known to themselves, they decline to answer.

That the petitioner, finding herself excommunicated from church privileges, without even a charge being made against her; condemned without trial, and left to suffer without cause and without redress; and being a poor female supporting herself by needlework to the utmost of her ability, with nothing to sustain her exertions but her moral integrity; she humbly and respectfully applied by petition, on 4th April last, to the Kirk Session for an explanation of the treatment she had received, and to be furnished with an extract of the Minute of Excommunication, and of the evidence on which it had proceeded; but her application was again disposed of as unworthy of notice. Upon which she protested and appealed to the Reverend Presbytery, and took instruments in the hands of the Session Clerk.

That the petitioner afterwards applied to the Session Clerk for an extract of the minute of said meeting of Session, which was promised but never furnished.

That the Rev. Mr Watson has since condescended to state to her *verbally*, that she will be restored to church privileges as formerly, provided she applies for the same as a probationer or young communicant.

That the treatment the petitioner has received from the Rev. Mr Watson and Mr James Hannan has not only been hurtful to her feelings, and prejudicial to her progress and exertions to support herself by honest industry, but is malicious and oppressive; and under the circumstances stated she is under the necessity of applying to the Reverend Presbytery for redress.

May it, therefore, please the Reverend Presbytery to sustain the petitioner's complaint—to call upon the Rev. Mr Watson and Mr James Hannan for an explanation of their treatment of the petitioner, and to produce the charge and evidence against her, upon which she has been excommunicated by them from church privileges without being heard in self-defence—to order extracts of said charge, evidence, and sentence of excommunication, to be furnished by the Session Clerk to the petitioner on payment of the usual fees, that the petitioner may be enabled to seek redress otherwise, if so advised; and in the event of their failing to do so, or there being no charge against the petitioner, then to find the conduct of the Rev. Mr Watson and Mr James Hannan towards her to be malicious, oppressive, and unchristian; and to censure the Rev. Mr Watson and Mr James Hannan accordingly, and restore the petitioner to the privileges of her *status* as a visible member of the church of Christ, and a communicating member of St Matthew's congregation. Or do otherwise, as the Reverend Presbytery shall think proper, according to justice.

The following letter from Rev. Dr Smith, Cathcart, contains the deliverance of the Presbytery:—

Copy Letter.

MANSE OF CATHCART,
3d October, 1854.

MADAM,—I regret that your note of the 18th ult. has been so long unanswered. It was delivered during my absence in England. The following was the deliverance of the Presbytery upon your petition at last meeting:— "The Presbytery took up the petition of Elizabeth Storie, who did not appear. Mr Watson having been heard on the subject, the Presbytery found that the petition is informal, but recommended the petitioner to renew her application, and submit herself in all meekness to the directions of the Kirk Session of St Matthew's, according to the laws of the Church."

I am,
MADAM,
Yours, etc.,
JAMES SMITH.

Mr Watson told a friend of mine at the Presbytery, that, as the case had been decided, he would expect to see me at his house. As recommended, I, in all meekness, went to Mr Watson's; but, instead of the courteous reception I anticipated, he told me he had nothing to say in the matter, and never thought I would come,—and saying this, he rang the bell with violence; but I calmly replied, that he would get no bells in heaven to ring for my departure. Before I reached the door he again rang with more violence. I then felt it to be my duty to lodge a representation with the Presbytery. The following is the representation to the Presbytery, October, 1854; and Dr Smith's letter which follows, contains the result of it:—

>Representation for Elizabeth Storie, in the application and appeal made by her to the Reverend Presbytery of Glasgow,
>Against the deliverance of the Kirk-Session of St Matthew's.
>The Representer is aggrieved by the deliverance of the Presbytery above quoted, and humbly begs to bring it under review—

Before farther remarks, the Representer will take the liberty of stating that, when she appealed to the Reverend Presbytery, she did not suppose that that Reverend Body would descend to any quibbling objection to the form of her complaint. Neither could she suppose that her application would be disposed of on the *ex parte* statement of her opponent, the Rev. Mr Watson; and above all, that the Reverend Presbytery would recommend her to renew her application to the Kirk-Session, so as to leave her to be dealt with by the very men she complained against.

On 3d October last, when her petition was taken up by the Presbytery, she was in attendance, but not wishing to be obtrusive, she took no prominent position; and her petition was taken up and disposed of on the statement of Mr Watson alone, without any opportunity for the Representer to be heard in reply.

Now, the Representer submits that her petition is not informal. It contains a pertinent statement of facts, relevant for probation, and true. The conclusions of the petition are properly and fairly deduced and supported, besides being reasonable in themselves, according to every rule of jurisprudence.

The Representer had already done everything in her power with the Kirk-Session to get redress, and their refusal to give it, compelled her to petition the Presbytery. But the Presbytery has thought proper, notwithstanding, to throw her back on the Kirk-Session, that her opponents may become her judges.

In appealing to the Reverend Presbytery, the Representer was led by the serious conviction that their single object would have been to ascertain the truth; and that whatever methods, consistent with equal justice to both parties, should seem best adapted for that end, that these methods would be pursued regardless of their conformity or non-conformity with the ordinary course, rules, and principles of procedure in civil courts of law; and her regret is only equalled by her astonishment that, although her petition is framed purposely to avoid any quibbling objection that might be taken hold of, still it has actually been disposed of on such an objection by a Reverend Presbytery, when no court of law in the kingdom would have listened to it for a moment.

The Representer, when a child, became the victim of experimental medical treatment, which has deprived her of the power of distinct articulation. This is her misfortune and not her fault. But the Kirk-Session overruled her application to be allowed to be heard by a friend, and the Reverend Presbytery has found her written statement informal. The Kirk-Session give no reason why they overruled her request, and the Reverend Presbytery are equally silent in what manner her petition is informal.

The Representer, as a visible member of St Matthew's Church Congregation, has been excommunicated without cause, insulted without giving any offence, and treated with malicious contumely by the Rev. Archd. Watson, minister, and Mr James Hannan, elder. And when she applies for redress, she is refused to be heard by the Kirk-Session; and on appealing to the Presbytery, she is told her complaint is informal, but recommended to submit herself in all meekness to the men who abused her, and whom she complains of. These facts the Representer states fearlessly, and trusts that the Presbytery may reconsider her case, recall their deliverance, hear both parties on her complaint, and award to the Representer an opportunity of proving her averments by the oath of the Reverend Archibald Watson and Mr James Hannan, or otherwise; and to these parties an opportunity of vindicating themselves and their conduct towards her.

There is surely nothing unreasonable in such a request. The charge is a grave one as regards the minister and elder, and a heartless, malicious, and injurious one as regards the Representer; and should the Reverend Presbytery again dispose of it on a quibble, the Representer shall, in justice to herself, appeal to the general public by a published statement of the whole facts.

In respect whereof.

(Copy of Letter.)

MANSE OF CATHCART,
15th Dec., 1854.

MADAM,—The Presbytery, at their last meeting, found that they could not entertain the Representation then made by you, both on account of its being disrepectfully worded, and of its having reference to a matter previously disposed of.

I am, MADAM,
Your obdt. Servant,

ELIZABETH STORIE.   JAMES SMITH.

The Representation, with the reasons for its rejection, are submitted to the ordeal of public opinion; and while I disclaim every intention of disrespect to the Presbytery, I cannot find, on reperusal of the document itself, anything disrespectful in it. It contains nothing but the truth, frankly and fearlessly stated. It is now before the reader, and left for him to judge whether there is anything disrespectful to justify the Presbytery in rejecting its reception. The other reason for rejection is startling and extraordinary, namely, that the Representation contains matter already disposed of. Of course it necessarily does; the very title, the very object, and the whole intention was to get the Presbytery to REVIEW what they had previously disposed of, and to correct the grievances they had entailed upon me. I was never aware, and have yet to learn, that the decision of a Presbytery Court of the Church of Scotland is, when once pronounced, to be held like the laws of the Medes and Persians, unalterable and irrevocable. But if this be so, then it clearly follows that the Representation was incompetent, and that the decision of the Presbytery should have been in accordance therewith.

I was present at the Meeting of Presbytery, October, 1854, but was not called on to make appearance; when I heard the unsatisfactory nature of the decision in regard to my representation, I took instruments, protested, and appealed to the Synod. Defeat never had the effect of daunting me—like George Stephenson, when striving to perfect his locomotive, his many defeats only stirred him up to renewed exertion, till he at last gloriously succeeded,—so every new defeat seemed to me just some new opportunity for exerting the little strength I had in the cause of right, hoping that at last I might succeed, and the cause of truth would triumph.

The first meeting of Synod was to take place in April, 1855; but before that time, it was published in the newspapers that Mr Watson was in ill health, and was not to preach for six months. He was going to the Continent. On his return, I received the following note at Ayr:—

Mr Watson has much pleasure in saying that the Session have accepted Miss Storie's explanation.

By presenting the enclosed ticket, properly filled up, Miss Storie will receive a token on Saturday, or on Sabbath morning.

177 West Regent Street, Glasgow.

I had never been asked by the Session, or any one connected with it, for an explanation. In fact, this is what I have been all along craving. As already shown, Mr Watson had been absent for several months. Upon his return, he, as Moderator, made a minute in the name of the Session, to the effect that the Session were satisfied with my explanation. So far from this being the truth, my answer from Ayr to Mr Watson's note of restoration, will show that this minute was made up in my absence. His note had no date, but my answer the following day is dated. The following is my reply:—

(Answer to the above.)

WELLINGTON SQUARE,
AYR, 27th October, 1855.

REV. SIR,—I humbly acknowledge receipt of your note, and enclosed communion cards, but I am sorry I will not be able to come home at this present communion, but I trust will be able to commune with the same spirit which is infused throughout. But I am glad to find that you at last have been convinced of your lack of duty and inability to cut off a member from the rights and privileges which in this life flow to believers, although the attempt has been to me a source of much grief, trouble, and expense.

I remain,
Yours accordingly,
ELIZABETH STORIE.

I was accordingly admitted once more a member of St Matthew's, and attended communion there in January, April, and October, 1856.

One of the painful results which followed the strange conduct of Mr Watson and his Kirk Session, appears from a letter that was sent to Mr Watson by a lady whom I had been occasionally employed by, to work for. She had heard of my name being removed from the communion roll, the truth and reason of which she wished to discover before employing me again; so she wrote to Mr Watson. The following is Mr Watson's answer:—

GLASGOW, October 13, 1856.

MY DEAR MADAM,—My absence from home for a few days has prevented me from answering your note sooner.

As you do not specify any particular charge which has come to your ears, respecting the individual referred to in your letter, I am unable to say anything about it. The proceedings of a Kirk Session are of course strictly private, so that I am hardly at liberty to mention what is done, or not done, in the case of any member of the church.

I believe, however, that where one has had the opportunity of testing the character of others, the safest and wisest plan is to act upon one's own experience, independently of all vague and unverified rumours.

Believe me,
Very truly yours,
(Signed)   ARCHD. WATSON.

Could anything more evasive, more cautious, or more insinuating be penned than this letter? Its mystification and implication is intended to make matters no better for me, while the over-anxiety to avoid self-committal on the part of the minister aroused suspicion that I had not been justly treated. Had I been guilty of anything to warrant the denial of church privileges, and to excommunicate me from the visible church, it was the reverend gentleman's duty to have warned her of the fact. Under the circumstances explained, she had a right to know the truth or untruth of the reports to my prejudice emanating from the proceedings of the reverend gentleman and his "strictly private" Kirk Session. But all she gets is a recommendation to judge of me by her own experience. It surely did not occur to him that I was entitled to the privilege of the same rule in laying before the world a published statement of the treatment I had experienced at the hands of him and others, and to constitute it judge betwixt us.

A friend of the poor and oppressed having heard of all the trouble, annoyance, and expense these proceedings of Mr Watson and the Kirk Session had needlessly cost me, asked Mr Hally to write to Mr Watson on the subject. The following is the letter which he wrote:—

(Copy Letter.)

GLASGOW, 28th Dec., 1855.

Rev. ARCH. WATSON,
177 West Regent Street, Glasgow.

REVEREND SIR,—A considerable time ago a friend of mine, who takes a generous interest in the poor and oppressed, asked me to inquire into a complaint of Elizabeth Storie, Bothwell Street, a member of your congregation, against unfeeling and injurious treatment received by her at the hands of you and Mr James Hannan, one of the elders of the church.

It is painful to reflect retrospectively on the annoyance, contumely, abuse, and injury this poor girl had to contend with, for no known reason, except her innocent physical misfortunes and helpless poverty. She could neither prevent the one, nor control the other, and was therefore compelled for a long time to remain in your hands, a struggling victim for Christian privileges, till her rights, so barbarously withheld, were acknowledged and restored. Little reflection will tell you how damaging church slander, and excommunication from church privileges, must be to a poor girl, with only her moral character, her needle, and public opinion to depend upon for her bread, and that a woman's character, at all times tender, when once assailed so formidably as hers has been by you, will retain, more or less, an everlasting blemish, notwithstanding her restoration to her *status* in the church. It must readily occur to you, that independent of her mental sufferings, and lack of bread, Miss Storie was put to considerable expense in actual outlay, besides loss of time travelling to attend, and kept hanging on Session and Presbytery meetings, from time to time, seeking redress so long denied her.

Miss Storie being now restored to her privileges, the merits of her complaint are admitted. But the matter does not end here. She is entitled to be reimbursed of her outlay—and to a reasonable amount,—as a *solatium* to her injured feelings; and I have been requested to see justice done to the poor girl in this respect;—but it is an unpleasant matter for me to enforce, and I therefore suggest that you should see Miss Storie personally, and arrange the matter at once, to prevent it going into Court, where every fact and circumstance will have publicity and notoriety, that can do Miss Storie no harm, and her opponents no good. It is your province to judge for yourself, and mine to do my duty, however unpleasant it may sometimes be.—I am, &c.,

(Signed) GEORGE HALLY.

In answer to this letter, Mr Hally heard from Mr Adam Paterson, one of the members of St Matthew's Kirk Session, saying that both he and Mr Watson appreciated the motive which dictated the letter, and requesting Mr Hally to call. When Mr Hally called on Mr Paterson, it was arranged that I should summon Mr Watson to the Small Debt Court for the sum of £12, to cover my expenses. When I was made acquainted with this arrangement, I disapproved of such a course. Some time after this, Mr Watson requested me to appear at a meeting of Session, to be held on 1st April, 1856, for the purpose of getting the whole matter adjusted, and expenses paid. I went accordingly, but nothing more was done. The minutes of the meetings, 4th April and 25th October, were read.

> At Glasgow, and within Saint Matthew's Session-House, the 4th day of April, 1854,
>
> At a meeting of the Kirk-Session of St Matthew's—Present, the Moderator, Mr Watson; Messrs Wylie, Hannan, M'Kinlay, M'Kay, Whyte, Collie, and Grant, Elders. Opened with prayer. Elizabeth Storie appeared and presented a petition to the Session, complaining of having been refused a token in October, 1853, although she had, as alleged in that petition, been a communicant from 1842 up till that date. The Session overruled a craving made by the applicant to be heard by a friend, whom she wished to introduce for that purpose. And having then heard the applicant with reference to the petition: They find they cannot entertain it, in respect the minister or elders, whether as a Session or individually, cannot deal with her application to have her name restored to the communion roll. Against this deliverance the applicant protested and appealed, and took instruments. Closed with prayer.
>
> (Signed)   ARCHD. WATSON, Moderator.

> 25th October, 1855.
>
> At a meeting of Saint Matthew's Kirk-Session, the Moderator reports that he having seen and conversed with Miss Storie, finds the cause of her absence having arisen from ill health, the Session thereby admits her name again to the communion roll.

I was then told the Session was perfectly satisfied that they had not made any charge against me, and there was none; therefore I had no claim upon them, as they had power to do as they thought proper with their members, and I ought to be satisfied and thankful that my name was again restored to the communion roll—this is the statement of Mr Watson and Mr Robertson. I replied that, on the very grounds that they had no charge against me, I had one against them for putting me to this trouble and expense. If I was punished for ill health, I thought I had the more need to be administered unto, or at least charged and tried for ill health, before being cut off the roll and thereby publicly exposed and left to the prejudice of all those who might take up an ill report against me. Mr Watson said, "Elizabeth, it will do you no good to take up these little matters." I thereupon lodged on the table a memorial of their former proceedings, (which is referred to in my letter to Mr Watson of 26th July, 1858,) and left. Mr M'Kinlay, an officiating elder, threw it out on the street after me; but as I wished them to look over their own proceedings, before I published them, I picked it up and slipped it in below the Session door to them. I called on Mr Adam Paterson next morning for an extract of said minutes, he stated that he had no further connection with St Matthew's Church, or Session, but sent me to Mr Watson for extracts, as he was at that time his own Session-Clerk. I was also to tell him that whatever farther he wished him to do as an agent he would do it, but nothing farther as a member of Session. I went to Mr Watson, delivered the message, and craved extracts. He asked me what I was going to do with them. I honestly told him I was going to defend myself by publishing them. He said I would only get them if I allowed no one to see them.

In January, 1857, I applied for a token to Mr Whyte, one of the members of St Matthew's Kirk Session, but was refused by him without any reason assigned, as on a former occasion in 1853. That day, and the following April, I communicated without a token. I have not since applied for a token; but on the occasion of the communion in October, 1857, and the three succeeding communions of that year, I filled up my name on one of the congregational communion slips, to prevent a renewal of the former wound to my feelings by being refused again.

I had intimated to Mr Watson that I had come to the determination to let the public know how I had been treated by those who are set in authority to be a terror to evil-doers, but a praise and protection to those that do well. Instead, however, of wishing to serve the cause of truth, by giving easy access to these documents, the only extract of a Kirk Session meeting I received, I was charged 10s. 6d. for.

> At Glasgow, and within Saint Matthew's Session-house, first December, 1857, at a meeting of the Kirk Session of Saint Matthew's,

Present—The Moderator, Mr Watson; Messrs Hannan, Whyte, Wylie, M'Kinlay, M'Kay, Collie, Grant, Robertson, Baird, Crawford, Carr, Balderston, Hay, and Ronald.

Opened with prayer.

The Moderator read to the Session the following letters from Elizabeth Storie, of No. 42 William Street, Glasgow, viz.: "23d November, 1857.—Rev. Archibald Watson, As I stated to you, some time ago, that I intended to publish a history of my life, but that before doing so I wished extracts from the minutes of St Matthew's Kirk Session, stating the cause of my excommunication. You admitted yourself that it would be a decided blank in the publication. For the last time I humbly appeal to you, as Moderator of St Matthew's Kirk Session, for the said extracts, and I shall pay the usual fee upon receiving them. The printer could not get on without them; and if I do not receive them on or before the 1st December, I will feel at heart sorry if I be under the necessity to take legal measures to force them, as I will immediately raise an action in the Court of Session, which will be incurred at the expense of you and the Session to find agents and counsel to defend you under your minutes, which you will there require to produce. As you maintain the right and power to excommunicate members without charge or trial, a short account was remitted the Editor of the *London Journal*, requesting him to find out and report from whence the authority came. I submit to you a copy of the *Journal*, with his answer, on page 208, 'J.E., Glasgow.' I trust when you read this it will bring you to a true sense of your presumption. I sincerely trust you will not allow the action to go on; however, it is your province to look to yourself. If you do allow it to go before the Court, the Presbytery will no doubt feel it their duty to give you a charge and trial for your conduct. I remain, a friend to truth, signed Elizabeth Storie, 42 William Street, Anderston." To be communicated.

(Signed) ARCHIBALD ROBERTSON.

"42 William Street, Anderston, Glasgow.—1st Dec. 1857. Rev. Archibald Watson, Rev. Sir, as I have received no answer from you to my letter of 23d ultimo, I humbly ask your permission to appear before the Session of St Matthew's to-night, that I may personally crave extracts from the minutes of that Session relating to my case. I will be there at a quarter-past seven o'clock, if I hear nothing from you to the contrary. Yours, signed Elizabeth Storie."

    (Signed)   ARCHIBALD ROBERTSON.

The Moderator laid upon the table the copy of the *London Journal* referred to in the above letter of 23d November, and read the extract referred to, viz.: "Nov. 28th, 1857, J.E. (Glasgow.) We think the whole case scandalous and absurd, and quite unworthy of parties making a Christian profession. We would advise your friend to let this matter drop, to shake off the dust of her feet against them, and to seek Christian communion elsewhere. We recommend her to join the church under the pastoral care of the Rev. David Russell, or the Rev. Mr Frazer."

The Moderator also read the following petition:—"1st December, 1857. Unto the Reverend the Kirk-Session of Saint Matthew's. The Petition of Elizabeth Storie, residing at 42 William Street, Anderston, Glasgow, Humbly Sheweth, that your Petitioner is desirous of having extracts from the minutes of St Matthew's Kirk Session, in so far as related to her, from June, 1853, or January, 1851. May it therefore please your respected Session to grant her the said extracts, according to justice. (Signed) Elizabeth Storie."

    (Signed)   ARCHIBALD ROBERTSON.

The Clerk thereupon stated that, on collecting the tokens at one of the tables at last communion, the said Elizabeth Storie, being seated there, handed him, instead of a token, a written memorandum (on one of the congregational communion slips) in the following terms:—

              "Pew No. 122.

    "Elder, ———

"Communicant's Name,   Residence,

  "Elizabeth Storie.   42 William Street.

"My reason in not applying for a token, is to prevent

a renewal of wounded feelings, as Mr Whyte, at the January Sacrament, 1857, renewed the former wound by refusing to give me a token.

"25th October, 1857."
(Signed) ARCHIBALD ROBERTSON.

The Kirk Session having duly deliberated, refused the prayer of the petition. Elizabeth Storie being called in, this deliverance was intimated to her; whereupon she protested and appealed to the Presbytery, took instruments and craved extracts, which were allowed. Closed with prayer.
(Signed) ARCHIBALD ROBERTSON.

The Session-Clerk's fee for this extract, 10s 6d.

(Copy Letter.)

ELIZABETH STORIE to the Rev. ARCHIBALD WATSON, 177 West Regent Street, Glasgow.

GREENSIDE PLACE,
EDINBURGH, 25th Dec., 1857.

REV. SIR,—I beg to intimate to you, as Moderator of St Matthew's Kirk Session, that at the next meeting of the Presbytery of Glasgow, to be held on the 6th proximo, a petition and appeal (containing reasons of dissent) will be presented at my instance against the decision come to by the said Kirk Session anent my application for church privileges.

I am,
REV. SIR,
Your most obdt. Servant,
(Signed) ELIZABETH STORIE.

At a meeting of Presbytery, within the Town Hall of Glasgow, held on the 6th day of January, 1858, Elizabeth Storie appeared, and lodged reasons of appeal, with extracts of minutes from St Matthew's Kirk Session, of 4th December, 1857, as desirous of having extracts from the minutes of St Matthew's Kirk Session, in so far as related to her, from June, 1853, or January, 1851. Mr Watson appeared for the Session, and Elizabeth Storie for herself. The decision of the Presbytery was, that as it was to complete the publication of the history of her life, they refused said extracts. Against this deliverance she took instruments, protested and appealed to the Synod of Glasgow and Ayr. Mr Watson acquiesced.

This decision will no doubt surprise many. No party requiring an extract minute of a Presbytery Court is bound to communicate the purpose it is required for; and the question readily suggests itself, viz., What had the Presbytery to fear from the published history of my life? and another, What motive had the Presbytery in suppressing their own proceedings from the test of public opinion?

The reasons of appeal to the Synod, with copies of Mr Watson's correspondence, along with medical and other certificates, were duly lodged within ten days after said meeting of Presbytery, with the Rev. Dr Smith of Cathcart, who is clerk for the Reverend Presbytery and Synod.

About six weeks before the meeting of Synod, I went to Dr Smith, at Cathcart Manse, to ascertain when it would be convenient to get the extracts of Presbytery, and also of the lodged documents. Dr Smith informed me that he had orders not to extract them, unless I paid him 1s 6d for each signature, as every page lodged would require to be signed by him as legal documents; the whole would amount to about £3, which he would be sorry to take from me, considering the weak state of body I was in, and my unfitness to work for it; but he would be obliged to get it, and take it beforehand, as he would in all probability be put upon oath if he had taken it; and it would be also useless, unless I got an able, honest man to plead my cause in the Synod, as I would not be heard myself.

The *animus* of the reverend gentleman and his coadjutors is here apparent. My poverty was well known to them, and was severe enough in itself without any aggravation at their hands. Nevertheless, see what use has been made of it by men who call themselves ministers of the gospel, and pretend to inculcate charity and benevolence as a Christian duty! No more effectual method could have been devised than that resorted to to frustrate the end of justice. But few men, it is hoped, would be found to descend to the degradation of such a heartless, demoralising act as the one recited. £3 was as formidable to me as £300. The Rev. Mr Watson and his friends knew the fact, took advantage of it, left me helpless, but themselves secure. My appeal to the Synod was thus forced to fall.

It is proper to state that the Rev. Mr Smith of Cathcart, and many others, uniformly treated me with becoming consideration and kindness.

I felt defenceless and unable to continue this unequal war, and thinking it would be beneficial to the Church's members, I have inserted the Presbytery's proceedings with the rest.

My reason for remaining in St Matthew's so long after the aforesaid treatment, was with the hope that Mr Watson would be led to see his errors, or at least left without excuse, and unable to bring any accusation against me, which his certificate now proves:—

It is hereby certified that Elizabeth Storie is, at this date, a member of the Established Church of Scotland, and leaves St Matthew's Congregation in full communion.

(Signed)   ARCHD. WATSON, Minister.

Glasgow, July 20, 1858.

---

42 William Street, Anderston,
GLASGOW, 26th July, 1858.

MR WATSON.

REVEREND SIR,—I acknowledge receipt of your certificate of church fellowship. This now closes our connection as minister and member, but as our other matters are not yet adjusted by you, I hold you, as minister, liable for the expenses incurred by me, (which have amounted to about £15 of outlay,) in consequence of your excommunicating me without charge or trial, contrary to the Word of God and the laws of the church. I have been treated by you in the same way as described in Ezekiel xxxiv. 4, as your conscience must bear witness. As it was stated at the close of the memorial I laid on the Session table, on the 1st of April, 1856, that if you did not make a speedy reparation for your aggression, I would feel it my duty, for the cause of truth as well as in justice to myself, to publish a full statement of the case with all your letters. Since that time many opportunities have been afforded you to do so, which you have not embraced. Now, a full history of my life is all written out ready to be published; your certificate and this letter will complete it. You remarked to me the other day, "that you believed whatever I took in hand to do I would do it right through, and that conscientiously."

In the strength of the Lord, who hitherto has upheld me, I shall endeavour to show that Christ has been my rock, my fortress, and my deliverer. If you have any answer to this letter, it must be sent to me on or before Friday first.

ELIZABETH STORIE.

(No answer.)

The reader will be anxious to know if my case in the Law Courts had advanced since 1853. When the Lord Provost refused to take any steps against their Town-Clerks, or those liable to them, and the Kirk Session refused to help me to force them to that step, I was, in these circumstances, under the necessity of letting the matter sleep for some time. So soon as I got a little stronger and able to work occasionally, I acted upon the advice Mr Meek had given me, namely, to save up Mr Kerr's allowance, raise an action, and compel production of the Burgh Court Books for 1823, and when the parties would be all in the field let each fight his own battle. My first step was to find agent and counsel. Mr Charles Scott, Sheriff-Advocate, agreed to act as my counsel; Mr Richard Arthur, S.S.C., as my agent. Both said it was a good case. After paying the court fees to Mr Arthur, he issued the summonses, and agreed to risk his own trouble on the merits of the case. The defenders all lodged defences, which were sent me to reply. My replies were minute and pointed, and I thought each defender was left without excuse. Mr Arthur did not lodge sufficient defences, but left it favourable to my opponents. Moreover, he never consulted Mr Scott, my counsel, although he led me to believe that Mr Scott was consulted all along— while all this time it was his son, an inexperienced youth. I learned this when too late. Mr Scott said Mr Arthur must have bungled the case, that he had never been consulted, nor seen a paper in it since the case went into court. I had the impression that Mr Kerr had followed me here also, and felt I must try and get a respectable agent to act with Mr Scott. I then got Mr D. T. Lees; and the following Record will show the proceedings adopted, and the result of the action.

The following certificate will show the condition I was in during all this warfare:—

(Copy Certificate.)

I hereby certify that Elizabeth Storie has applied to me, for the purpose of obtaining my opinion as to the performance of an operation for her relief. The jaws are firmly united to each other in great part of their extent, and the mouth is closed so as scarcely to admit of a goose-quill.

Her statement that her present condition is the result of the injurious use of mercury during childhood, is, I have no doubt, quite correct. I believe she may obtain some relief from an operation.

(Signed) RICHARD JAS. MACKENZIE, F.R.C.S.E.

Edinburgh, 31 Abercromby Place,
    February 24, 1852.

Doctors Lawrie and Corbett recommended that this operation should be postponed, as a last resource, as my strength would never stand it.

From the time that the jaw gave way in April, 1854, I suffered great pain occasionally, until Nov., 1856, when the coupling of the jaw-bone gave way, and lodged in the glands. Dr Corbett attempted twice that day to get it out, but the opening of the mouth was so small, it could not even be seen. Inflammation ensued, and the pain I suffered for ten days is indescribable. Barm and linseed meal poultices took away the inflammation; then, by perseverance with a probe, I managed to bring it to the front of the mouth, but under the tongue. I went to Dr Corbett, and said, Whatever requires to be done, you must take this out. The Doctor made several attempts to get hold of it, but it was so much larger than the opening, that it always slipped back; at last our efforts were crowned with success, and it was brought to the top of the tongue. The Doctor then saw that it was impossible to take it out without enlarging the opening, except he could snip the bone in pieces; but then there was the danger of cutting the tongue. He introduced a flat probe, which I held to keep down the tongue, while he snipped the bone in pieces; even then there was great difficulty in getting them out. It is impossible to express the relief this afforded me; indeed, I had never known what it was to breathe freely, since Falconer's treatment, until now. This coupling was a part of the burnt jaw-bone which Dr Corkindale removed in 1823, and so filled the space and pressed the tongue as to render speech painful and indistinct. Since then, I speak better, and am able to take more solid food.

APPENDIX.

First Division.

April 29, 1857.

RECLAIMING NOTE—ELIZABETH STORIE,

AGAINST

Lord Ardmillan's Interlocutor.

D. T. LEES, S.S.C., Reclaimer's Agent.

CAMPBELL & SMITH, S.S.C.,
WOTHERSPOON & MACK, S.S.C., } Defenders' Agents.

Mr CURRIE, Clerk.

Edinburgh, 19th March, 1857.—The Lord Ordinary having heard counsel for the parties, and made avizandum, and considered the closed record, productions, and whole process—Finds, 1*st*, That the pursuer has not averred facts relevant and sufficient to sustain the conclusions of the action against the defenders Mr Davie and Mr Turner, and assoilzies them accordingly from the conclusions of the action, and decerns: Finds, 2*d*, That the pursuer has at the bar judicially declined to state whether she admits or denies the genuineness and validity of the receipt, bearing to be dated 2d October, 1823, and to be subscribed " J. Christie for A. Malcolm," No. 15 of process, while the defenders, Mr Cross and Mr Kerr, aver the authenticity of that receipt; and finds that if the said receipt is authentic, there is no relevant ground of liability set forth against Mr Cross: Therefore assoilzies the defender Mr Cross from the conclusions of the action, and decerns: Finds, 3d, That the pursuer has not alleged that the process mentioned on the record is in the possession, or within the controul, of the defender Mr Kerr, nor that it is in his power to restore or recover the same, nor that the same has been lost by him, or by any person for whom he is responsible: Finds that, under the circumstances disclosed by the pursuer on record, there are no grounds relevant to support the conclusions for restoration of the said process against Mr Kerr as the foundation of the relative conclusions for damages against him; therefore assoilzies the defender Mr Kerr from the conclusions of the action, and decerns: Finds the defenders entitled to expenses, allows accounts thereof to be given in, and when lodged, remits the same to the auditor to tax and report.

(Signed)   JAS. CRAUFURD.

Note.—The Lord Ordinary thinks that this action, brought after the lapse of above thirty years, to compel discovery and restoration of this old process, or to recover damages from the defenders, is, on the pursuer's own shewing, quite groundless. The old process is on all hands admitted to be irrecoverable, and the action is truly for damages. But the pursuer has not, in regard to any of the defenders, laid a relevant case for damages. The defenders explained that they did not strongly press for expenses, and it is understood that the claim will probably not be enforced. But as they may be involved in further litigation, expenses have been awarded.

(Initialed)   J. C.

Unto the Right Honourable the Lords of Council and Session,

RECLAIMING NOTE

FOR

ELIZABETH STORIE, residing at No. 9 Bothwell Street, Glasgow;

IN THE

ACTION at her instance against JOHN KERR, writer in Glasgow, the surviving partner of the late Firm of Malcolm and Kerr, or Kerr and Malcolm, writers there; ANDREW CROSS, some time writer in Glasgow, now Sheriff-Substitute of the Western District of Perthshire, and residing at Dunblane, the surviving partner of the late Firm of Young and Cross, writers in Glasgow; and WILLIAM DAVIE, Esq., and ANGUS TURNER, Esq., the Town-Clerks of the Burgh of Glasgow and Barony of Gorbals of Glasgow;

Humbly Sheweth,

That in this case Lord Ardmillan, Ordinary, was pleased, of this date (March 19, 1857), to pronounce the foregoing interlocutor, which is now submitted to the review of your Lordships.

May it therefore please your Lordships to recal or alter the said interlocutor submitted to review; to find that the reclaimer was entitled, in the circumstances, to call all the defenders as parties to the action; that she is not hoc statu *bound to make her election between them, but is entitled to have the facts investigated, and the defenders discussed in such way and in such order as may appear advisable; and that she has stated a relevant and sufficient case to that effect; and to remit to the Lord Ordinary to proceed with the cause; or to do farther or otherwise in the premises as to your Lordships shall seem proper.*

According to Justice, &c.

CHAS. SCOTT.

INDEX TO RECORD.

	Page
1. Summons,	122
2. Revised Condescendence for Pursuer, and Revised Defences for Defenders,	124
3. Statement of Facts for Cross and Kerr, and Answers for Pursuer,	131
4. Statement of Facts for Davie and Turner, and Answers for Pursuer,	136
5. Plea in Law for Pursuer,	142
6. Pleas in Law for Cross and Kerr,	142
7. Pleas in Law for Davie and Turner,	143
8. Interlocutor closing Record,	144

RECORD.

1.—SUMMONS.

VICTORIA, etc.—Whereas it is humbly meant and shown to us by our lovite, Elizabeth Storie, residing at No. 9 Bothwell Street, Glasgow, *pursuer*, against John Kerr, writer in Glasgow, the surviving partner of the late firm of Malcolm and Kerr, or Kerr and Malcolm, writers there; Andrew Cross, sometime writer in Glasgow, now Sheriff-Substitute of the western district of Perthshire, and residing at Dunblane, the surviving partner of the late firm of Young and Cross, writers in Glasgow; and William Davie, Esq., Angus Turner, Esq., and Arthur Forbes, Esq., the town-clerks of the burgh of Glasgow, and barony of Gorbals of Glasgow, *defenders*, in terms of the condescendence and note of pleas in law hereunto annexed: Therefore the defenders ought and should be decerned and ordained, by decree of the Lords of our Council and Session, conjunctly and severally, or according to their respective liabilities, to produce and make forthcoming to the pursuer, a process of damages which was instituted in or about the year 1823, and subsequently for some time depended in the court of the burgh of Glasgow and barony of Gorbals of Glasgow, at the instance of the pursuer, and her father, John Storie, as her administrator-in-law, since deceased, against William Falconer, surgeon, then residing in Glasgow, and now residing in Paisley, in which the pursuers concluded for damages to the extent of £1000 sterling, with interest and expenses, and of which process the said William Davie, Angus Turner, and Arthur Forbes, as town-clerks foresaid, were the legal custodiers, and the said Malcolm and Kerr, or Kerr and Malcolm, of which firm the said John Kerr is the surviving partner as aforesaid, acted as agents for the pursuer, and her said father as her administrator-in-law, and the said Young and Cross, of which firm the said Andrew Cross is the surviving partner, and as agents for the said William Falconer therein, and in which process the pursuer ultimately obtained decree against the said William Falconer for the sum of £1000 in name of damages, with interest and expenses of process as concluded for, or at least the pursuer would have obtained such decree therein, and which process is illegally withheld from the pursuer, or otherwise; and in the event of the said process being withheld and not made forthcoming to the pursuer, the defenders ought and should be decerned and ordained, by decree foresaid, conjunctly and severally, or according to their respective liabilities, to make payment to the pursuer of the sum of £1000, in name of damages, and as a *solatium* for the loss and injury sustained by her, by and through the want of said process, and the withholding thereof from the pursuer as aforesaid, all as set forth in the condescendence hereunto annexed; and in either event the defenders ought and should be decerned and ordained, conjunctly and severally, to make payment to the pursuer of the sum of £100, or such other sum as our said Lords shall modify as the expenses of the process to follow hereon; conform to the laws and daily practice of Scotland, used and observed in the like cases, as is alleged.—OUR WILL IS, etc.

Summons signeted 29th October, 1855.

2.—Revised Condescendence for Pursuer; and Revised Defences for the Defenders.

Cond. Art. 1. In the year 1823 the pursuer and her father, John Storie, then residing in Tradeston, Glasgow, since deceased, as her administrator-in-law, (she being then in minority,) instituted an action before the court of the burgh of barony of Gorbals, Glasgow, against William Falconer, surgeon, then practising in Glasgow, and now in Paisley, concluding for damages to the extent of £1000 sterling, with interest and expenses of process therein mentioned.

Answer for Cross and Kerr, 1. Admitted, with reference to the defenders' statement, that in the year 1823 the action here referred to was raised by the pursuer in the court of the burgh of barony of Gorbals. There is no such court as that of the "burgh of Glasgow and barony of Gorbals."

Answer for Davie and Turner, 1. Admitted that in the year 1823 the pursuer, who sued in *forma pauperis*, had an action in dependence at her instance against William Falconer before the court of the burgh of barony of Gorbals. *Quoad ultra* not known to the defenders, and not admitted.

Cond. Art. 2. The said damages were claimed on account of injuries inflicted on the pursuer's person by the reckless and unskilful use of mercury and aquafortis on the part of the said William Falconer, and which were of the most serious and permanent character, and resulted in a union of the jaws, whereby the pursuer has been deprived of the power of taking solid food, (the orifice of the mouth being so close as to admit only of the barrel of a quill), and subjected to the most excruciating pains and suffering in her person, and been rendered unfit to do anything for her maintenance and support, which state of existence she has endured for upwards of thirty years. She has also during that period undergone no fewer than nineteen operations of a most painful description, by eminent surgeons of Glasgow, in the expectation of obtaining some relief to her sufferings, but without effect.

> *Answer for Cross and Kerr*, 2. Admitted that damages were claimed in said action on grounds similar to those here mentioned, but the averments here made relative to a period subsequent to the raising of the said action, and therefore not embraced therein, are denied.

> *Answer for Davie and Turner*, 2. Not known to the defenders, and not admitted.

Cond. Art. 3. To the action of damages before mentioned, the said William Falconer lodged defences, and after a variety of procedure therein, and his undergoing a judicial examination, decree for damages, interest, and expenses of process, which has long since become final, was pronounced against him, in terms of the conclusions of the summons; at all events the pursuer would have obtained such decree if the process had not been illegally withheld as after mentioned.

> *Answer for Cross and Kerr*, 3. Admitted that the action was defended, and that the pursuer sought, and, of this date, (Sept. 19, 1823,) obtained, an order of court, appointing Mr Falconer to be judicially examined. This was the last Interlocutor in the cause. Admitted that the examination took place, with this explanation, that Mr Falconer's statement on examination was negative of the grounds of action, and that the pursuer thereafter took no further steps in the

case, and the action was dropped. *Quoad ultra* this article is denied.

Answer for Davie and Turner, 3. Denied, except that, as appears from the minute-book, the defender, in the action referred to, was, on the 19th September, 1823, appointed to undergo a judicial examination, which was the last interlocutor pronounced in the cause.

Cond. Art. 4. While the said process was in dependence, the said William Falconer absconded from Glasgow, and was not heard of by the pursuer for a number of years. She at length, however, discovered that he was, and had been for some time, resident and practising as a surgeon in Paisley, and was in circumstances to enable him to liquidate her claims.

Answer for Cross and Kerr, 4. Admitted to the effect that Mr Falconer went to Paisley, where, in the knowledge of the pursuer, he resided, practised his profession, and was in good circumstances. *Quoad ultra* this article is denied.

Answer for Davie and Turner, 4. The defenders believe that Falconer went to Paisley, and became resident there. *Quoad ultra* not known to the defenders, and not admitted.

Cond. Art. 5. With the view of obtaining a settlement thereof, the pursuer applied to the defenders, William Davie, and Angus Turner, and Arthur Forbes, (now deceased,) the town-clerks of the burgh of Glasgow, and barony of Gorbals, for an extract of the decree pronounced in her favour in the foresaid process, or at least for the said process itself, but they denied all knowledge of the case. The pursuer also applied to the other defenders, John Kerr and Andrew Cross, for restoration of said process, or for such information as might lead to the discovery and procuring thereof, but could get no satisfaction from them.

Answer for Cross and Kerr, 5. Admitted that the pursuer recently applied to each of the present defenders for the process in question, but not till after the subject-matter of it had been settled in another action of damages raised by the pursuer, on the same grounds, against Mr Falconer. The alleged applications to the town-clerks about the said process are not admitted. *Quoad ultra* this article is denied.

Answer for Davie and Turner, 5. Denied that any decree was pronounced in the process, or that the pursuer applied for the process to the present defenders. Neither they nor Mr Forbes, who has died since he was cited as a defender in this action, were appointed town-clerks until many years after the process was borrowed. At that time the town-clerks were the late Mr James Reddie and Mr Robert Thomson.

Cond. Art. 6. At length, after advertising for the said process, which was alleged to have been lost, in the Glasgow newspapers, and making other fruitless attempts to recover the same, the pursuer was advised to submit a representation of her case to the Lord Provost and Magistrates of the city of Glasgow. This was accordingly done, of this date, (Jan. 7, 1853,) which led to an examination of the burgh court books, where it was found that a receipt for said process had been given by "J. Young for Andrew Cross," dated 22d September, 1823. This was communicated to the pursuer, with an excerpt from the minutes of a meeting of the magistrates, held of this date, (Jan. 19, ———,) to the following effect:—"That as the "town-clerks have a receipt for the process which "depended before the magistrates of Gorbals by a

"party legally entitled to borrow the proceedings, and
"to grant the receipt, there is no just cause of com-
"plaint against the town-clerks, and that the magi-
"strates must decline to interfere in the matter."

> *Answer for Cross and Kerr*, 6. Not known to the defenders, and not admitted, that the pursuer advertised for the process in the Glasgow newspapers. Admitted that in the beginning of 1853, nearly thirty years after the process had been borrowed, a letter on behalf of the pursuer was written to the Lord Provost of Glasgow about the process—that the receipt for the process, dated in September, 1823, which was contained in the receipt-book for processes kept by the extractor of court, and is patent to all litigants, was produced to the magistrates, and that the quotation in the article under answer is an extract from a minute of the magistrates on the subject. Reference is made to the minute itself, and to the pursuer's letter. *Quoad ultra* not known and not admitted.

> *Answer for Davie and Turner*, 6. Not known to the defenders, and not admitted, that the pursuer advertised for the process in the Glasgow newspapers. Admitted that in the beginning of 1853, nearly thirty years after the process had been borrowed, a letter on behalf of the pursuer was written to the Lord Provost of Glasgow regarding her process, that the receipt for the process in September, 1823, was produced to the magistrates, and that the quotation in the article under answer is an extract from a minute of the magistrates on the subject.

Cond. Art. 7. The process having thus been traced to the defender Andrew Cross, application was made to him to return the same, but instead of doing so, he, to her great disappointment, sent the pursuer a copy of a receipt which he pretends to hold for said process, signed by "J. Christie for A. Malcolm," of date the 2d October, 1823, being ten days subsequent to his receipt for the same which stands in the burgh court books. The above named "A. Malcolm" was the partner of the defender John Kerr, the survivor of Kerr and Malcolm, or Malcolm and Kerr, and for whose acts he, as the surviving partner, is responsible, and although the pursuer applied to Mr Kerr for said process, he denied all knowledge thereof, and declined to give her any satisfaction.

Answer for Cross and Kerr, 7. Admitted that application having been made to Mr Cross on the part of the pursuer to return the process, he stated and now avers, that he had it not—that he gave it up to the pursuer's own agent, Mr Malcolm, in 1823, upon a receipt dated 2d October, 1853, a copy of which was sent her. Admitted that Mr Malcolm, now deceased, was a partner of the defender Mr Kerr. Admitted that Mr Kerr informed the pursuer that he was not possessed of the process, and did not know where it was. *Quoad ultra* denied.

Answer for Davie and Turner, 7. It is believed that the process was borrowed from the defenders' agent in the cause by Mr Malcolm, a partner of Kerr and Malcolm, who were the pursuer's own agents therein. *Quoad ultra* not known to the present defenders, and not admitted.

Cond. Art. 8. The pursuer thereupon applied to the defenders William Davie, Angus Turner, and Arthur Forbes, the town-clerks of the burgh of Glasgow and barony of Gorbals, to force back said process from the defender Andrew Cross, under his receipt of 22d September, 1823, but they declined to issue a caption for the return of said process, or to take any steps under said receipt, in respect he was not resident within the jurisdiction of the Court.

> *Answer for Cross and Kerr*, 8. It is believed that recently a verbal application was made to Mr Simson, the extractor of Court, for a caption against the defender, Mr Cross, for return of the process, and that Mr Simson, in the circumstances, declined to issue such a caption. *Quoad ultra* not known and not admitted.
>
> *Answer for Davie and Turner*, 8. It is denied that the pursuer applied to the present defenders for a caption against Mr Andrew Cross, but believed that she, or an agent for her, made a verbal application for such caption to Mr Simson, the extractor of Court, which he declined to give, and reference is made to the defenders' statement for the grounds of such refusal.

Cond. Art. 9. The pursuer is still without said process. It has been illegally withheld from her, and the defenders, or one or other or more of them, are bound to produce and make the same forthcoming to her.

> *Answer for Cross and Kerr*, 9. Denied, in so far as the present defenders are concerned. They are not in possession of the process, and notwithstanding that every exertion has been made to discover it, they have been unable to discover any trace of it.
>
> *Answer for Davie and Turner*, 9. This article is denied in so far as the present defenders are concerned.

Cond. Art. 10. By and through the want of said process, and the illegal withholding and retention thereof by the defenders, the pursuer has already sustained, and will yet sustain, serious loss, injury, and damage; and in the event of their failing to make said process forthcoming, they are jointly and severally, or according to their respective liabilities, bound to make her suitable reparation as aforesaid; and although she has repeatedly called upon them, and each of them, either to produce to her the said process, or to make her such reparation, they have refused, at least delayed so to do, and the present action has become necessary.

Answer for Cross and Kerr, 10. Admitted that the pursuer has threatened the defenders with all manner of proceedings, civil and criminal, and that she made various demands upon them for money, with which they refused to comply. *Quoad ultra* denied.

Answer for Davie and Turner, 10. Denied that the pursuer has sustained or can sustain damage from the want of the process, and reference is made to the defenders' statement.

3.—STATEMENT OF FACTS FOR DEFENDERS, CROSS AND KERR, AND ANSWERS FOR PURSUER.

Statement 1. To the pursuer's action against Mr Falconer, raised in 1823, the defence was a denial of the grounds of action. In accordance with the practice of the times, which in Glasgow was favourable to judicial examinations in most cases, an interlocutor, dated 19th September, 1823, was pronounced, appointing Mr Falconer to undergo a judicial examination, which accordingly he did undergo, with this qualification and explanation, that his statements were negative of the grounds of action. No proof was led, and no interlocutor was given or pronounced affecting the merits of the suit. The order for judicial examination was the last interlocutor in the cause, and the suit was allowed to drop.

Answer 1. Admitted that the action referred to was raised, and that Mr Falconer underwent a judicial examination. *Quoad ultra* denied.

Statement 2. The defender, Mr Cross, holds the receipt of Mr Malcolm, the pursuer's agent, for the process, dated 2d October, 1823. It is signed by Mr J. Christie for Mr Malcolm, Mr Christie being at the time Mr Malcolm's authorised clerk. The small memorandum on receipt-book containing the receipt is produced.

Answer 2. Denied.

Statement 3. In the year 1849, the pursuer raised another action against Mr Falconer before the Sheriff of Renfrewshire, on the same grounds with the foresaid action raised in 1823, and having substantially the same conclusions. This action was defended by Mr Falconer. A record being made up between the parties, a proof taken, and parties heard, the Sheriff-Substitute, of this date, (Oct. 15, 1850,) pronounced an interlocutor, in which he "assoilzied the defender from the conclusions of the libel, and decerned," finding the pursuer liable in expenses. This judgmen was affirmed by the Sheriff. A note of advocation on the part of the pursuer was then presented in the Court of Session, which resulted in a judgment of the Lord Ordinary (Handyside), of this date, (Jan. 19, 1855,) repelling the reasons of advocation, remitting the cause *simpliciter* to the Sheriff, and finding the respondent, Mr Falconer, entitled to expenses. This judgment is now final.

Answer 3. Denied.

Statement 4. In December, 1851, the pursuer,

through Mr J. M. Macqueen, then one of the agents for the poor, applied to this Court, as appears from the minute-book, under date, (31st January, 1852,) "for the benefit of the poor's-roll, to enable her to "carry on law-suits at her instance, against William "Falconer, surgeon, residing at No. 6 Neilson Street, "Paisley, James Reddie, town-clerk, Glasgow, Andrew "Cross, Sheriff-Substitute in Dunblane, and John "Kerr, writer in Glasgow." The application having been remitted to the reporters on the *probabilis causa*, they reported against the application, which was accordingly refused by the Court, on the 5th March, 1852. The action which the pursuer then proposed to raise was based on the same grounds, and was substantially the same with the present action, except that she proposed to include in it as defenders her former opponent, Mr Falconer, and also Mr Reddie, then principal town-clerk, while Messrs Davie, Turner, and Forbes, who were not town-clerks when the pursuer's process was borrowed, were not to be included.

Answer 4. Admitted that the pursuer applied for the benefit of the poor's-roll, and was refused the same. *Quoad ultra* denied.

Statement 5. Soon after her application for the benefit of the poor's-roll had been refused, a person styling himself Dr William Macdonald, wrote a letter on the pursuer's behalf to the Lord Provost of Glasgow, in which it was stated that the pursuer's process of 1823 "has been illegally retained or wilfully de- "stroyed by the town-clerks," and praying that they "should be ordained to make the same forthcoming, "or that warrant of incarceration be granted against "them." The Lord Provost, of this date, (Jan. 19, 1853,) submitted this application to the magistrates, and after having taken into consideration the receipt for the process, granted to the extractor by the defenders' agent, Mr Cross, and the subsequent receipt to Mr Cross by the pursuer's agent, also the subsequent action which she had raised before the Sheriff of Renfrewshire, in which the defender was assoilzied, together with the result of the application for the benefit of the poor's-roll, the magistrates were of opinion that there was no just cause of complaint against the town-clerks, and that they must decline to interfere in the matter. They made a minute to this effect, and directed an extract of it to be sent to Dr Macdonald. A certified extract of this minute is in process.

Answer 5. The application is admitted, under reference thereto. *Quoad ultra* not known and not admitted.

Statement 6. The pursuer then applied by petition for redress to the Secretary of State for the Home Department, which was remitted, through the medium of the Lord Advocate, to the procurator-fiscal of the Burgh Court of Glasgow, that he might inquire into the circumstances and report. His report was equally unfavourable to the pursuer, with that of the reporter on the *probabilis causa.* The pursuer accordingly received no countenance or encouragement from the Home Secretary.* The letter from the Crown-Office

---

* WHITEHALL, 29th April, 1853.

SIR,—I am directed by Viscount Palmerston to acknowledge the receipt of your letter of the 4th instant, enclosing a Petition from Elizabeth Storie, in which she complains of the unjust detention of a process to which she was a party: and I am to inform you, that upon inquiry the complaint appears to be unfounded.

I am,
SIR,
Your obedient Servant,
W. WADDINGTON.

Mr Robt. Storie,
15 Bothwell Street, Anderston, Glasgow.

in Edinburgh to Mr Burnet, procurator-fiscal, sending him the copy of the petition to the Secretary of State, and the copy of the petition itself, are produced in process.

Answer 6. Admitted, under reference to the petition and letter referred to.

Statement 7. The pursuer's next step, was to present, through a new agent for the poor, Mr William Montgomerie, W.S., another application for the benefit of the poor's-roll, to enable her to raise an action. Mr Reddie having died in the interval, the action was now proposed to be brought against Mr Davie, Mr Turner, and Mr Forbes, as the then town-clerks, without including Mr Falconer, Mr Cross, or Mr Kerr. Intimation was appointed of this new application, as appears from an entry in the minute-book, of this date, (Feb. 25, 1853). The reporters on the *probabilis causa* having again reported against the pursuer, the application was refused, as appears from an entry in the minute-book of this date, (May 27, ——).

Answer 7. Admitted, under reference to the application and report here mentioned.

Statement 8. After this second application for the benefit of the poor's-roll had been presented, and before it was disposed of, the Lord Provost of Glasgow again received various letters from the same Dr William Macdonald, on the subject of the pursuer's case, which his Lordship submitted to the magistrates, of this date (May 16, 1853), when, after reference to their minute of 19th January preceding, and to the unsuccessful application to the Secretary of State, the magistrates again declined to interfere in the matter, and directed that a copy of their minute to this effect should be transmitted to Dr Macdonald, with a request that he would abstain from troubling the Lord Provost any farther in the matter. An extract of the minute is produced.

Answer 8. Admitted, under reference to the application and minute here mentioned.

Statement 9. It is believed that the pursuer sometime ago made a verbal application to Mr Simson, the present extractor of the burgh court, for a caption to be initialed by him that it might be signed by a magistrate, against Mr Cross, for recovery of the process, but Mr Simson, in the circumstances above detailed, declined to accede to the application. The pursuer did not present any written application to the magistrates against either Mr Cross or Mr Kerr to make the process forthcoming.

Answer 9. Not known whether the applications here referred to were made, and therefore not admitted.

4.—STATEMENT OF FACTS FOR DAVIE AND TURNER, DEFENDERS, AND ANSWERS FOR PURSUER.

Statement 1. The defenders personally know nothing of the action of damages which the pursuer states she brought against William Falconer in the burgh court of Gorbals. But it appears from the act book of that court that a process was brought in June, 1823, at the instance of "*Poor* Elizabeth Storie (the present pursuer) against William Falconer," that certain pleadings were ordered, and a proof allowed, and that the last interlocutor in the cause, which was dated 19th September, 1823, appointed the defender to undergo a judicial examination. A certified excerpt of all the entries in the act book relative to the process, is produced.

Answer 1. Admitted that a proof was allowed and taken, and that a judicial examination was undergone by Mr Falconer. *Quoad ultra* not known and not admitted.

Statement 2. In that process Messrs Kerr and Malcolm, writers in Glasgow, the surviving partner of which firm is Mr John Kerr, who has been called as a defender, were the pursuer's procurators, and Mr Andrew Cross, then writer in Glasgow, now Sheriff-Substitute at Dunblane, and who has been also called as a defender, was the defender's procurator.

Answer 2. Admitted that the defender Mr Kerr was the pursuer's procurator, and that the defender Mr Cross was Mr Falconer's procurator.

Statement 3. On the 22d September, 1823, being three days after the date of the last interlocutor, the process was borrowed by the defender's procurator, Mr Cross, from Mr John Fisher, now deceased, who was then the extractor of Court, and who took a receipt for it from Mr Cross's clerk. The extractor is the officer who has the custody of all the processes before the burgh courts, and attends to the borrowings and returnings. This is no part of the town-clerks' duty, their time and services being otherwise fully engaged. The process was never returned to the extractor's office, and the receipt by the defender, Falconer's agent, still remains. But the defenders were informed and believe—and indeed it is stated by the pursuer herself—that the process was afterwards borrowed by her own agent, Mr Malcolm, whose receipt Mr Cross still holds. An excerpt from the process receipt-book, containing the above-mentioned receipt by Mr Cross, certified by the present extractor, is produced.

Answer 3. Admitted that a receipt by Mr Falconer's agent still stands for the process. Denied that the pursuer ever stated that the process was borrowed by Mr Malcolm. *Quoad ultra* not known and not admitted.

Statement 4. In December, 1851, the pursuer, through Mr J. M. Macqueen, S.S.C., then one of the agents for the poor, applied to this Court, as appears from the minute-book, under date 31st January, 1852, "for the benefit of the poor's roll, to enable her to "carry on law-suits at her instance against William "Falconer, surgeon, residing at No. 6 Neilson Street, "Paisley, James Reddie, town-clerk, Glasgow, Andrew "Cross, Sheriff-Substitute in Dunblane, and John "Kerr, writer, Glasgow." The application having been remitted to the reporters on the *probabilis causa*, various papers were laid before them, and among others, a process which the pursuer had not long before brought in the Sheriff Court of Renfrewshire against William Falconer, then a surgeon in Paisley, of the same nature as the process which she had raised against him in 1823, before the burgh court of Gorbals, and in which second action, all objections to its competency having been waived, and a proof having been led, the defender Falconer was, of this date (October 15, 1850), assoilzied by the Sheriff on the merits,[*] and an advocation of that judgment afterwards in this Court dismissed with expenses, of this date (Jan. 19, 1855). The reporters on the *probabilis causa* having reported against the application for the benefit of the poor's-roll, it was refused by the Court on the 12th March, 1852, as appears from an entry in the minute-book of that date. The action which the pursuer then proposed to raise was of the same

---

[*] See Kerr's letter to Mr Stewart, S.S.C., Edinburgh, p. 57.

nature, and was to be based on the same grounds as the present action, except that she proposed to include in it as defenders, the said William Falconer and Mr Reddie, then principal town-clerk, while the present defenders and Mr Forbes, who were not town-clerks when the pursuer's process was borrowed, were not to be included.

Answer 4. Admitted that the application here referred to was made. *Quoad ultra* not known and not admitted.

Statement 5. Soon after her application for the benefit of the poor's roll had been refused, as mentioned in last article, a person styling himself Dr William Macdonald, wrote a letter on the pursuer's behalf to the Lord Provost of Glasgow, in which it was stated that the pursuer's process, which had been borrowed by her own agent from the defender's agent, Mr Cross, in 1823, "has been illegally retained, or "wilfully destroyed, by the town-clerks, and praying "that they should be ordained to make the same "forthcoming, or that warrant of incarceration be "granted against them." The Lord Provost, of this date (Jan. 19, 1853), submitted the application to the magistrates, and after having taken into consideration the receipt for the process granted to the extractor by the defenders' agent, Mr Cross, and the subsequent receipt for the process to Mr Cross, by the pursuer's own agent, the new action which she had raised before the Sheriff of Renfrewshire, and in which, after a proof, the defender was assoilzied, together with the result of the application for the benefit of the poor's-roll, the magistrates were of opinion that there was no just cause of complaint against the town-clerks, and that they must decline to interfere in the matter. They made a minute to this effect, and directed an extract of it to be sent to

Dr Macdonald. A certified extract of this minute, from which the pursuer has made a short quotation in her condescendence, is produced.

Answer 5. The letter and minute here mentioned are admitted, under reference to their terms. *Quoad ultra* not known and not admitted.

Statement 6. The pursuer then applied by petition for redress to the Secretary of State for the Home Department, which was remitted through the medium of the Lord Advocate to the procurator-fiscal of the burgh court of Glasgow, that he might inquire into the circumstances and report. His report was equally unfavourable to the pursuer, with that of the reporters on the *probabilis causa*, and accordingly the pursuer received no countenance or encouragement from the Home Secretary. The letter from the Crown Office in Edinburgh to Mr Burnet, procurator-fiscal, sending him the copy of the petition to the Secretary of State, and the copy of the petition itself, are produced.

Answer 6. The petition and letter here mentioned are admitted, under reference to the documents themselves.

Statement 7. The pursuer's next step was to present, through a new agent for the poor, Mr William Montgomerie, W.S., another application to the Court for the benefit of the poor's-roll, to enable her to raise her action. Mr Reddie having died in the interval, the action was now proposed to be brought against the defenders, Mr Davie, Mr Turner, and Mr Forbes, as the then town-clerks, without including Mr Falconer, Mr Cross, or Mr Kerr. Intimation was appointed of this new application, as appears from an entry in the minute-book of this date, (Feb. 25, 1853.) The reporters on the *probabilis causa* having again reported against the pursuer, the application was refused, as appears from an entry in the minute-book of this date, (May 27, ——.)

Answer 7. Admitted that the application here referred to was made. *Quoad ultra* not known and not admitted.

Statement 8. After this second application for the benefit of the poor's-roll had been presented, and before it was disposed of, the Lord Provost of Glasgow again received various letters from the same Dr William Macdonald on the subject of the pursuer's case, which his Lordship submitted to the magistrates, of this date, (May 16, ——,) when, after reference to their minute of the 19th January preceding, and to the unsuccessful application to the Secretary of State, the magistrates again declined to interfere in the matter, and directed that a copy of their minute, to this effect, should be transmitted to Dr Macdonald, with a request that he would abstain from troubling the Lord Provost any farther in the matter. An extract of the minute is produced.

Answer 8. Admitted, under reference to the documents here mentioned.

Statement 9. The defenders believe that some time ago the pursuer by herself, or an agent, made a verbal application to Mr Simson, the present extractor of the burgh court, for a caption to be initialed by him, that it might be signed by a magistrate, against Mr Cross, to recover the process which he had borrowed in 1823, but had afterwards lent to the pursuer's own agent, Mr Malcolm, and that Mr Simson declined to issue a caption in the circumstances which have been now detailed. The pursuer did not present a written petition to the magistrates against Mr Cross and Mr Kerr, one or other of whom, she says, is bound to make the process forthcoming, so that they might have had an opportunity of explanation, but preferred to raise the present action of damages against them and the present defenders, as now the town-clerks.

Answer 9. Not known and not admitted.

5.—PLEA IN LAW FOR THE PURSUER.

In the circumstances set forth in the revised condescendence, the defenders are bound to make the process in question forthcoming to the pursuer, or otherwise to pay her damages, in terms of the conclusions of the summons with expenses, and the pursuer is entitled to decree accordingly.

In respect whereof.

(Signed)　　　RICHARD ARTHUR.

6.—PLEAS IN LAW FOR MESSRS CROSS AND KERR.

1. The pursuer has stated no relevant ground of action against the present defenders, or either of them.

2. The pursuer having by her agent received the process in question from Mr Cross, the action is totally groundless as against him.

3. It is also groundless in other respects, both as against Mr Kerr and Mr Cross, who have not the process, and are unable to make it forthcoming. There is no ground in law or equity for subjecting them in damages.

4. The pursuer has no interest to call for delivery of the process—1*st*. In respect it was virtually abandoned or superseded by the subsequent action raised against Mr Falconer before the Sheriff of Renfrew-

shire, in which Mr Falconer was assoilzied.* 2*d*, In respect that the judgment in the action before the Sheriff of Renfrewshire forms a *res judicata* with respect to the merits of the process called for; and 3*d*, In respect the process called for can be of no use, avail, or value to the pursuer.

5. In the circumstance of the case there has been such *mora* as disentitles the pursuer to sue.

6. With reference to the circumstances set forth, the defenders are entitled to have the action dismissed, or otherwise to have absolvitor with expenses.

In respect whereof.

(Signed) N. C. CAMPBELL.

7.—PLEAS IN LAW FOR MESSRS DAVIE AND TURNER.

1. The pursuer has stated no relevant ground of action against the present defenders.

2. The allegations of the pursuer being in all essential respects, as regards the present defenders, ill founded in fact, the action cannot be maintained against them.

3. The defenders are unable, and are under no obligation to make the process in question forthcoming to the pursuer, nor is there any ground in law or equity, either alleged or truly existing, for subjecting them in damages to her.

4. The pursuer has no interest to call for delivery of the process referred to, as it could be of no use to her, having been entirely superseded by the similar action which she afterwards brought before the Sheriff

---

* The reader's attention is drawn to Mr Kerr's correspondence with the different agents.

of Renfrewshire, and in which the defender was assoilzied on the merits.

5. The defenders are entitled to have the action dismissed, or otherwise to absolvitor with expenses.

In respect whereof.

(Signed) R. MACFARLANE.

8.—INTERLOCUTOR CLOSING RECORD.

5th June, 1856.—Lord Ardmillan.—*Act.* Arthur, *Alt.* Macfarlane.—Declares the record closed on the revised condescendence, and revised defences, Nos. 16, 13, and 17 of process, and appoints parties' procurators to debate, reserving to all the parties to make productions within eight days.

(Signed) JAS. CRAUFURD.

On 28th May, 1858, the Lords of the Second Division refused to hear counsel, and sustained the decision of the Lord Ordinary.

CONCLUDING REMARKS.

On appeal to the Inner House of the Court of Session, the decision of the Lord Ordinary was adhered to on 28th May, 1858, and thus finally decided the case in the Supreme Court of Scotland, leaving me with the alternative of an appeal to the House of Lords, or to submit to the decision pronounced.

It may be presumptuous in me to state my conviction that the decision is contrary to reason and equity; but the most eminent judges are but men subject to the fallibility of human nature.

On reference to what lawyers call the *ratione decidendi*, that is, the reasons on which a decision is given, stated in the note appended to the decision itself, it will be observed that delay in raising my action is held to leave my claim groundless. Other reasons are stated, but delay is the fundamental and paramount one. Had the note stopped with the remark on delay, the decision would have been, if not more just, at least more intelligible. But another reason, viz., that the old process being admitted on all hands to be irrecoverable, and that the present action was truly one for damages, while I had not, in regard to any of the defenders, laid a relevant claim for damages, is stated as a secondary but conflicting reason for relieving the defenders from damages.

With regard to the delay, there is no doubt it was great, and that the inconvenience of it to my opponents, and hardship of it to me, were unfortunate facts for all concerned in the issue of my action, excepting Dr Falconer, the author of all my grievances, but to none so great as to myself, and of all others it should not have been imputed to me.

At the time the old process was raised against Dr Falconer, I was a helpless child. Shortly afterwards I was bereaved of my father, and left an orphan, without any one to interest themselves in the prosecution of the case—depressed by permanent bodily suffering—deprived of the power of speech—disfigured and disabled in appearance by medical experimental abuse—subjected to the contumely of the thoughtless, wanton, inconsiderate, and unfeeling, and still, with any strength I had, compelled to struggle for my bread—time was unavoidably lost; but no opportunity within my power was ever neglected in my exertions to recover the old process, and compel redress.

After being tossed about from Mr Kerr, my agent, to the Town-Clerks, from these gentlemen to Mr Cross, and from that gentleman back upon Mr Kerr, I found myself involved in a desperate struggle between might and right, affluence and poverty, self-importance and insignificance, with no other backing than perseverance, and years of toil and trouble, and considerable expense; besides, a host of difficulties had to be overcome before I found myself able to stand at the bar of the Supreme Court of Scotland, seeking justice, where I had always been led to believe there was no respect of persons, and that, poor and helpless as I was, justice would be accorded me. But here I stood alone, a helpless female, opposed to the city clerks of Glasgow, a district Sheriff of a neighbouring county, and an intelligent writer in Glasgow.

After the legal forms of the Court had been gone through, the learned judges found everything I had done, positive and negative, to be insufficient to support my action; assoilzied the whole defenders, and found me liable in expenses; the primary reason for this decision being, because the learned Lords *think* that after such a lapse of time I am not entitled to redress. My orphanage, minority, poverty, physical distress—my persevering, ceaseless efforts, are all left out of view and disregarded; and although I never allowed one hour's delay in my efforts to arrive at the position I then stood in, still I was thrown out of Court because the learned Lords think I am not entitled, after such a lapse of time, to any redress at their hands. Had I had the good fortune to have the prefix of "Countess" or "Lady" to my name, or had my opponents been as poor and unimportant as myself, it is possible, I think, their Lordships would have given the case more consideration, and perhaps have pronounced a different decision.

The second reason, viz., the old process being irrecoverable, my case resolved into a claim of damages; but that I had not, in regard to any of the defenders, laid a relevant case for damages, has never been reconcileable with the fact. It is true that the case, in the event of the old process being withheld, resolved into a claim of damages, and the summons is framed purposely to meet the alternative that, in the event of the process being withheld, the defenders ought to be ordained conjunctly and severally, or according to their respective liabilities, to make payment to me of £1000, in name of damages, as the loss I sustain by withholding the process from me, the adjudication of the amount to be imposed upon the party or parties to blame, being left to the Court to fix, according to the respective liabilities of the parties.

I think the reader will be ready to admit that the

party withholding the old process, and thereby preventing me from recovering my claim against Dr Falconer, was bound to indemnify me; and seeing that the defenders implicated one another, they were all properly brought into Court together, that the parties to blame might be made accountable according to their respective liabilities. This was giving all of them an opportunity of vindicating themselves, and fixing the liability on the proper party.

To have selected any one or more as defenders would have been unfair to the others, besides being precarious to my own interest. The question was clearly one of responsibility among the parties themselves, and it is not said that I was bound to make any selection.

The alternative conclusion I was entitled to insist on; and its relevancy is indisputable in a case where it is admitted that my property is withheld from me by parties who were responsible for its restoration.

The learned judges, however, think that, for the reason given in the note to the decision, I am not entitled to my property, nor to any equivalent, and refuse both. But this is not all the hardship.

The concluding remarks of the learned Lord's note are worthy of grave consideration, viz.: "The defen-"ders explained that they did not strongly press "for expenses, and it is understood that the claim "will not probably be enforced; *but as they may be* "*involved in farther litigation, expenses have been* "*awarded.*"

It would have been more consistent with the sanctity of the law and dignity of the judge, to have refrained from such a remark; and had either the one or the other been consulted, it would never have been written.

The evident object of finding me liable in expenses is an attempt to manacle the hands of justice, and deprive me of every remaining opportunity to establish my legal rights by farther litigation. Had my opponents pressed for expenses, and the learned judge been called upon to deal with them, his duty would then have been to do so. But in the face of my opponents disclaiming expenses, the judge forces a decree into their hands, to protect them against any farther attempt on my part to vindicate my rights by appeal to a higher tribunal, where his decision would be subjected to review.

It may be difficult for me to divest myself so fully of partiality in judging in my own cause, as to enable me to form an unprejudiced opinion. It is difficult also to apply the principles of jurisprudence to the particular circumstances of disputed questions, and reconcile the result with justice to all parties involved;

and therefore, while I will not impugn the decision of the learned judge on the one hand, I cannot on the other convince myself of the justice of it, or reconcile the reasons on which it is founded with any principle of law or equity. My claim to redress is not denied, but it is refused *because I have been unable to make it sooner.*

These remarks may not be altogether thrown away. The oppression of the weak by the powerful is a law of nature in unceasing operation; and there may be many indulging in hope of redress from the laws of their country for flagrant wrongs endured by them, ready to embark in litigation with powerful opponents. But they will do well to consider the bitterness they may be doomed to suffer in the result—not from justice, but from the administration of what is so called in the Supreme Courts of their country. It is a proverbial saying, that "a friend in Court is worth a penny in the purse," and more than me are no doubt ready to subscribe to the remark.

It is seen that, from a healthy child, I have been doomed to a life-time of misery by a young medical practitioner, whose object may have been to gain fame by an experimental discovery. It can hardly be supposed that either vindictiveness or maliciousness could have avenged itself on an unoffending child of my age at the time; but whatever may have been the motive, there is no doubt of the effect. I am the victim, doomed to a life-time of suffering and misery without redress.

Happiness in this world to me has long been annihilated, but life is supportable through the Christian hope of the world to come—while pain, poverty, and bitterness are my constant attendants. Few of those who have been born in affluence, and brought up in luxury, or others who enjoy the blessing of health and energy to contend with the world, will be impressed by this narrative of my sufferings; but the afflicted like myself will not withhold their sympathy.

As a professing Christian and member of the visible church, I found consolation in the celebration of its ordinances; and while health permitted me to attend and participate in the holy sacrament of the Lord's Supper, and confess myself an unworthy sinner, accepting and acknowledging my Saviour's love to fallen mankind, I did so. But, as if my cup of bitterness was not full enough already, this Christian privilege was denied me, and my name expunged from the roll of communicants. Without anything being laid to my charge, without my knowledge, and without any reason being assigned, I was excommunicated, and left to contend with the consequences.

My sufferings were great, my misfortunes many, my friends few, but my moral character had never till then been impeached, either directly or by implication; my integrity was all I had to depend on for my bread, and this I was now to be robbed of by a minister of the gospel and his Session Court, without assigning any reason for doing so.

In seeking relief, when a child, from a simple complaint incident to children, and easily cured, I was made the victim of experimental medical abuse, and left to drag out a miserable existence, borne down with pain and poverty.

In seeking consolation from the ordinances of religion, I have been denied and deprived of them; and in seeking redress from the laws of my country, from the authors of my misery, it has been refused me. A living victim of the three learned professions—Medicine, Law, and the Church; with bodily infirmity, physical weakness; dependent on my needle for my bread, to drag out a miserable existence, I leave in the hands of the reader this narrative of my sufferings, with an ardent hope that it may be the means of interesting the sympathy of those who have the power to exert it in favour of the oppressed against their oppressors; and I trust, for the sake of humanity, there may be none doomed to suffer all the misery inflicted on me.

Like the box of Pandora, one comfort remains for me that all the world cannot deprive me of—the consolation of God's Word in the present world, and the hope of happiness in the world to come.

ERRATUM.

Page 22, 14th line from top, in a few copies, *for* "an aged and diseased woman," *read*, "an aged woman, afflicted with disease of the heart."

LIST OF SUBSCRIBERS.

Margaret Murray, Springfield Court,	1 Copy.
George Hally, 43 Dalhousie Street,	2 "
D. T. Lees, S.S.C., Edinburgh,	1 "
George M'Nab, 30 Brown Street,	1 "
Wm. M'Donald, M.D., 359 Argyle Street,	1 "
Mrs George Smith, 21 Elmbank Place,	1 "
Robert Meikle, Hazeldean, Mearns,	1 "
James Hamilton, Newton, Mearns,	1 "
Robert Sweenie, 2 Gilmour Place, Rutherglen Road,	1 "
Miss Campbell, Seymour Lodge, Cove,	1 "
John Campbell, Knockderry, Cove,	1 "
John Bell, 36 West Russell Street,	1 "
Mrs Muir, Partick,	2 "
Mrs Macintosh, Elderslie Street,	1 "
Miss Ann Clarke, at Mrs Bell's, Holland St.,	1 "
Mrs Bodstein, 108 Peel Terrace, Garnet Hill,	1 "
Duncan Hilston, M.D., Great Helmsly, York,	1 "
James Hilston, Lanark,	1 "
Hugh Lindsay, Covington, Mains,	2 "
Miss Gibson, 6 Bank Street, Hillhead,	3 "

LIST OF SUBSCRIBERS.

A. G. Corbett, 6 Bank Street, Hillhead,	2 Copies
Thomas Corbett, Dowanhill,	2 "
Mrs Ebbels, Partick,	2 "
David Smith and James Davie, 42 William Street, Anderston,	2 "
ohn Barr, 42 William Street, Anderston,	1 "
Robert M'Nee, 30 William Street, Anderston,	1 "
Mrs James Campbell, Stobcross Street,	1 "
Jessie Brown and Mary Irvine, 21 Elmbank Place,	2 "
Jessie M'Lean and Ann Clarke, 15 Fitzroy Place,	2 "
Miss Murdoch, 9 Sandyford Place,	1 "
Miss Galloway, 108 Douglas Street,	1 "
Miss Ewing, 135 Sauchiehall Street,	1 "
Mrs M'Kail, 5 Martyr Street, Townhead,	1 "
Miss Tennant, Greenvale Place, Woodside Road,	1 "
Miss M'Call, 155 Renfrew Street,	1 "
Mrs John M'Call, Quebec,	1 "
Mrs Laurie, Partick,	1 "
Miss Mitchell, 15 Bothwell Street,	1 "
Alexander Watson, 15 Bothwell Street,	1 "
Margaret Watson, 15 Bothwell Street,	1 "
Mrs Williamson and Miss Bruce, 15 Fitzroy Place,	3 "
Mary Cameron and Mary M'Call, 2 Clifton Street,	2 "
Sarah and Margaret Cameron, 26 St Vincent Street,	2 "

LIST OF SUBSCRIBERS.

John Ross, 1 Main Street, Partick, - - 1 Copy.
Mrs Dr Robertson, 1 Newton Street, - - 1 "
Miss Leitch, Rutherglen Road, - - - 1 "
Miss A. Miller, 21 Elmbank Place, - - 1 "
John Hamilton, 15 Bothwell Street, - - 1 "
Miss Agnes M'Kechnie, 16 St Vincent Terrace, 1 "
Miss E. Allen, Dow Hill, by Girvan, Ayrshire, 1 "
Miss M'Murty, Bourtree Park, Ayr, - - 1 "
Duncan Cameron, Helensburgh, - - - 1 "
Robert Richard, St Vincent Crescent, - - 1 "
Mr Jackson, Douglas Street, - - - 1 "
Mr Murray, Buchanan Street, - - - 1 "
An Old Friend, - - - - - - 1 "
A Friend, - - - - - - - 2 "
Mrs Davidson, North Street, - - - 1 "
L. Carmichael, Calton Street, Edinburgh, - 1 "
Mrs Patrick Mitchell, Lyndoch Street, - 3 "
Mr Robert M'Farlane, Bridge of Weir, - 1 "
Rev. Mr Gilmour, Greenock, - - - 1 "
Mrs Wardrop, Beith, - - - - - 1 "
William Cuthbert, 64 Howard Street, - - 1 "
D. Miller, 5 Buchanan Street, - - - 1 "
William Wood, 5 Buchanan Street, - - 1 "
J. C. Small, 5 Buchanan Street, - - 1 "
John Hodge, 5 Buchanan Street, - - 1 "
Mrs Roberton, 45 East Bothwell Street, - 1 "
Mrs Heugh, Holmhead Street, - - - 1 "
Mr Carmichael, druggist, Edinburgh, - - 1 "
Miss Anderson, Sauchiehall Street, - - 1 "
Thomas Phillips, 43 Dalhousie Street, - - 1 "

LIST OF SUBSCRIBERS.

Alex. Moncrieff, advocate, 16 Cumberland Street, Edinburgh,	1 Copy.
Agnes M'Cormick, 11 Royal Terrace,	1 "
Mrs Copland, Helensburgh,	1 "
Miss Cochrane, 83 Renfield Street,	1 "
Miss Marion Muir, Newton, Mearns,	1 "
Miss Kessock, 6 Main Street, Anderston,	1 "
Mrs J. C. Bruce, Newcastle,	1 "
Mrs C. Brown, 1 Newton Street,	1 "
Isabella M'Kinnon, 1 Newton Street,	1 "
Mr James Buchanan, S.S.C., George Street, Edinburgh,	1 "
A Reverend Friend,	1 "
Miss Anderson, 16 Greenside Place, Edin.,	1 "
Mary Bowie, Mr Gibson's, 16 Royal Crescent,	1 "
Mr Peter Falconer, 73 Macalpine Street,	1 "
Mr James Stewart, 75 Macalpine Street,	1 "
John Scott, Terry Street,	1 "
Mrs Orr, Green,	1 "
Ann Patton,	1 "
John Hart,	1 "
Elizabeth Lawson, 26 Buckingham Terrace,	1 "
James Smith, 123 Dundas Street,	1 "
J. & A. Wylie, 28 Muslin Street,	1 "
Lillias M'Intyre, 2 Corn Street,	1 "
Mrs Brodie, Shandon,	1 "
Richard Verry, St Vincent Crescent,	1 "
Margaret M'Kenzie, Fitzroy Place,	1 "
Miss Ritchie, Lyndoch Street,	2 "
Mrs Clapperton, 12 Buckingham Terrace,	1 "

Margaret Lees, 12 Buckingham Terrace, - 1 Copy.
Mrs Millar, 2 Gilmour Place, - - - 1 "
Mrs Wood, Lanark, - - - - 1 "
Dr Dougan, 89 Cambridge Street, - - 1 "

www.ingramcontent.com/pod-product-compliance
Lightning Source LLC
LaVergne TN
LVHW061215060426
835507LV00016B/1947